Gulf Gothic

ANTHEM STUDIES IN GOTHIC LITERATURE

Anthem Studies in Gothic Literature incorporates
a broad range of titles that undertake rigorous, multi-disciplinary
and original scholarship in the domain of Gothic Studies
and respond, where possible, to existing classroom/module needs.
The series aims to foster innovative international scholarship
that interrogates established ideas in this rapidly growing field,
to broaden critical and theoretical discussion among scholars and
students, and to enhance the nature and availability
of existing scholarly resources.

Series Editor
Carol Margaret Davison—University of Windsor, Canada

Gulf Gothic

Mexico, the U.S. South and La Llorona's Undead Voices

Dolores Flores-Silva and Keith Cartwright

ANTHEM PRESS

Anthem Press
An imprint of Wimbledon Publishing Company
www.anthempress.com

This edition first published in UK and USA 2023
by ANTHEM PRESS
75–76 Blackfriars Road, London SE1 8HA, UK
or PO Box 9779, London SW19 7ZG, UK
and
244 Madison Ave #116, New York, NY 10016, USA

British Library Cataloguing-in-Publication Data
A catalogue record for this book is available from the British Library.

Library of Congress Cataloging-in-Publication Data
A catalog record for this book has been requested.

ISBN-13: 978-1-83998-0-367 (Pbk)
ISBN-10: 1-83998-0-362 (Pbk)

Cover credit: Cover painting Miguel Angel Cime Ku

This title is also available as an e-book.

CONTENTS

ACKNOWLEDGMENTS

We would like to thank our anonymous reviewers, as well as Carol Margaret Davison, and especially Virginia Stewart, for responses that improved the quality of this book.

Parts of Chapter 2 appear in a different version in "Faulkner and Modernist Gothic," *The New William Faulkner Studies*, edited by Sarah Gleeson-White and Pardis Dabashi (2022), 36–50, published by Cambridge University Press.

Our research for this project was supported by a Roanoke College Summer Research Fellowship and a Fulbright-García Robles award with Universidad de las Américas Puebla (UDLAP) in Mexico.

For readers interested in further interaction with topics addressed in this study, please see a series of films featured on our website: short documentaries on a group of Maya poets in Yucatán, the legacy of a maroon community in Veracruz, and traditions of honoring the dead on All Saints Day in Louisiana have much to add to the *Gulf Gothic* conversation. We thank Michael Boyles for his work in maintaining the site: https://gulfsbetweenus. domains.unf.edu.

Finally, we are immensely grateful for the cover artwork by Miguel Angel Cime Ku (of Yucatán) painted for this project by request. And we thank Maya Cartwright for her rendering of "Monument 32" from the Tamtoc site on the border between San Luis Potosí, Veracruz, and Tamaulipas.

Introduction

GULF GOTHIC

It was the third day of the seventeenth month;
the long count was 8.5.3.3.5, and the day was 13 Snake.
A sun-eating moon took place;
piercingly the bludgeon star [Venus] had shone earlier, late in the day.

> —from the La Mojarra stela in epi-Olmec script,
> dated 8.5.17.15.2 (157 AD)
> Terrence Kaufman and John Justeson, "Epi-Olmec Hieroglyphic
> Writing and Texts"

The Gulf, your gulf, is daily widening [...]

> —Derek Walcott, "The Gulf"

Along the Gulf of Mexico, over three thousand years ago, people were changed, domesticated by a species (*Zea mays*) they had been domesticating. Imagine a maize-matrix, on the coast and river basins of northern Tabasco and southern Veracruz, through which maize began to write itself and use its hosts to reproduce: trefoil signs like a fleur-de-lis, two leaves with a cob in the middle coming out of a man's head. Maize lost the ability to self-propagate, was dependent on humans for survival, but as Michael Blake makes clear, "by becoming habitual users," humans became "both the cultivators and the cultivated" in a "biosocial entanglement" that brought them into hierarchical urban societies to nurture a plant that was changing in symbiosis with them (21–22). An elaborate set of Olmec ritual arts was organized around this botanical mother–father in whose service people became children of the corn. "Here we shall inscribe, / we shall implant the Ancient Word, / the potential," the K'iche' Maya *Popol Vuh* tells us in a book of origins that opens—in Dennis Tedlock's translation—with the ritual language of laying out a cornfield (63), and moves through several creations and apocalypses until arriving at "the modeling of our first mother-father, / with yellow corn, white corn alone for the flesh" (146). Mesoamericans had long been bioengineering corn. The Gulf Olmec societies mark a moment of urban flowering when the Maize-god had refashioned humankind.

Sets of observations about seed and harvests, astronomical phenomena, time and space, had to be communicated across generations to set the conditions for city-states to emerge in the Olmec heartland between Tabasco and Veracruz—starting with San Lorenzo (1200–800 BC), La Venta (800–400 BC), and Tres Zapotes (400 BC–AD 100). Mesoamerican glyphic writing likely developed and proliferated in this Gulf culture, along with the long count of years (with its zero point of origin: August 11, 3114 BC) and additions to the calendar. The oldest lengthy text scholars think they can read, the Mojarra stela, contains 577 glyphs in twenty-one columns of Epi-Olmec script and narrates the reign of Harvester Mountain-Lord from a date marked as May 21, AD 143 (Beverido Duhalt 36). From even the most conventional academic perspectives, we could say that American literature starts here, in this monument's claims on power, projected into a future for which it would be ancestral. But American writing stretches further back than this four-ton text pulled from the Aula River of Veracruz in 1986 near the Olmec site of Tres Zapotes. Discovery of the Cascajal block, unearthed near San Lorenzo, extends the Gulf archive another millennium to 1000 or 900 BC: the serpentinite tablet holds sixty-two glyphs, including four different glyphs associated with maize (Blake 195). We are called, however, to wider considerations. While Tedlock's 2010 anthology of Maya literature presents a two-thousand year literary corpus, Paul Worley and Rita Palacios' *Unwriting Maya Literature: Ts'íib as Recorded Knowledge* (2019) challenges literary confines by affirming "the Maya category ts'iib over constructions of the literary," presenting "a multimodal Indigenous understanding of text" that includes and exceeds the "colonial legacy of alphabetic literacy" (3). Similarly expansive, Gloria Elizabeth Chacón's *Indigenous Cosmolectics: Kab'awil and the Making of Maya and Zapotec Literatures* (2018) draws upon the "double gaze" of dialogic creation presented in the *Popol Vuh*—"heart of sky, heart of earth," Huracán and Plumed Serpent (15)—while observing that in the K'iche' Maya version the term for this sacred "vision that duplicates" (13), that creates and transmits, is "*kab'awil: ka* (the numeral two) and *wil* (to see)" (15). Any deep vision of writing from the Gulf exceeds received categories of colonial letters and engages this multimodal vision that reproduces, including textiles, earthworks, the design of rows in the cornfield, spoken word and embodied performance, as well as the logographic and syllabic signs used in Mesoamerican writing. American writing starts here in the double gaze of the human–maize symbiosis.

Whether we begin with histories of maize and writing, Spanish conquest or the rapacious rise of the plantation system, the shores of the Gulf of Mexico make for a cross-cultural ground zero of modern North America. Rarely, however, is the Gulf examined as a transnational region (taking in the Gulf states of Mexico and the US, as well as western Cuba), with key ports in Veracruz, New Orleans, and Havana. The Gulf—from its loop currents to its Mississippi, Rio Grande, and Usumacinta basins—is a space of contact zones, creolization, and passages and impasses between peoples. It extends out into the Caribbean as a Greater Gulf, and through migration into the North American interior and beyond. For us, the Gulf signifies metaphorically and symbolically, as well as topographically. Lowercase "gulfs"—gulfs between peoples—bear an explosive charge that demands to be addressed in relational form through a dialogic set of long perspectives, and a doubled vision or consciousness. This is very much the terrain of gothic: the anxieties, displacements, and engulfments surrounding our stories, "ghosting" our national and professional discourses and their "choice[s] of exclusion and inclusion of historical events," as Enrique Ajuria Ibarra has pointed out (135) in slightly different context in his essay "Ghosting the Nation: La Llorona, Popular Culture, and the Spectral Anxiety of Mexican Identity."

Gulfs between Us

There is a regional unity to the Gulf of Mexico that has been obfuscated by national narrative. Jack Davis's Pulitzer Prize winning *The Gulf: The Making of an American Sea* (2017) offers a political and environmental history that addresses only the Gulf's US shores. The lacunae of such a framework carry pernicious staying power in our time of border hysteria. Matthew Pratt Guterl's *American Mediterranean: Southern Slaveholders in the Age of Emancipation* (2008) reaches into both the Gulf and the Caribbean. Still, Guterl's *American Mediterranean* is one held and policed by US American power. Cuban historians attend more fully to Spain's long presence in the Gulf and Caribbean as Arturo Sorhegui's "La Habana-Veracruz: El Mediterráneo Americano y el circuito imperial hispano, 1519–1821" (2002) conveys. Our approach aligns with Dalia Antonia Muller's "The Gulf World and Other Frameworks" (2018), which emphasizes "the unique connectedness of the space in and in between Mexico, Cuba, and the United States" and argues that a Gulf framework may help us see "nothing less than a shared history that remains in the shadow spaces between our bounded national histories" (18). Since gothic is the literary genre most attached to "shadow spaces," our charting of a Gulf Gothic navigates these triangulated waters even as we focus primarily on Mexican and US Gulf shores. We draw on the historiography and anthropological work of Mexican scholars: Andrés Latapi and Claudio Vadillo López's *Historia Ambiental de la Región del Golfo de México* (2019), Sara Ladrón de Guevara's *Culturas del Golfo* (2012), and the collaborative perspectives collected in Nancy Marie White's *Gulf Coast Archaeology: The Southeastern United States and Mexico* (2005) as we attend to Gulf gothic(s) and undead gulfs.

Of course the modern Gulf—taking shape in the wake of Cortés, the slave trade, and the plantation—precedes the gothic. But a consciousness that gave rise to gothic consciousness emerged here. In his early history, *La Florida* (1605), Inca Garcilaso de la Vega presented the *criollo* as a term invented by Africans to acknowledge gulfs of orientation between enslaved African parents and their children born in the Americas (106). Like most everything else related to African authority, Europeans soon appropriated the term to refer to their own (white) children born in the colonies. Three modern Caribbean writers who thought deeply about these issues guide our sense of what's at stake in listening to the Gulf's undead voices. In *Poétique de la relation*, Édouard Glissant described how enslaved Africans were transported through a "gulf matrix" *gouffre-matrice* (18) of Middle Passage into forced *fréquentation du gouffre* or "gulf frequentation" on plantations and in port cities where a "Whole-world knowledge" (20) took shape. Guyana's Wilson Harris wrote similarly of "Creoleness" and how, "within the gulfs that divide cultures [...] there exists [...] a storage of creative possibility that, once tapped, may energize the unfinished genesis of the imagination" (235). We can certainly see the gothic nature of those openings and impasses welling up in a poem like Derek Walcott's "The Gulf" (1969), as it points to accelerating damages wrought by post-plantation systems of wealth extraction: "down every coast where filling station signs / proclaim the Gulf, an air, heavy with gas, / sickens the state, from Newark to New Orleans" (107). Walcott's poem carries dread prophetic force: "The Gulf, your gulf, is daily widening" (107).

European gothic may be a by-product of colonialism and of the moral and intellectual decadence that was companion to Enlightenment structures of thought, especially charged in the Anglo-Protestant world. If maize changed people, so too did easy money and steady repression of gulf-guilt: sugar, tobacco, coffee, cacao, cotton, indigo, and rice produced on a plantation scale with enslaved labor. Jesus' message to the Pharisees about "a great gulf fixed" as impasse between the living and the dead (*Holy Bible*, Luke 16.26) found application to racialized gulfs between the living and the socially dead. Thus, Atlanta *Constitution* editor Henry W. Grady could draw on civic faith to assert that "the caste of race has set an impassable gulf" in a Dallas speech (1888) defending slavery's white supremacist afterlife (34). Much of our political history circulates in these loop currents. Across the Gulf, Mexico's founding fathers moved to abolish "the caste of race," with Morelos—who may have worn his signature bandanna to cover the African texture of his hair—announcing in "Sentiments of the Nation" (1813) that "slavery is proscribed forever, as well as distinctions of caste [...] the only distinction between one American and another shall be that between vice and virtue" (190). Through Mexico's long, caste-tinged battles between liberals and conservatives, a more catholic mode of white (or *criollo*) supremacy emerged. Drawing from New Spain's eighteenth century *casta* paintings and their hierarchical taxonomies of racial types, José Vasconcelos's *The Cosmic Race* (1925) asserts: "The lower types of the species will be absorbed by the superior type [...] and in a few decades of aesthetic eugenics, the Black may disappear" (32). In this manner, via a *mestizaje* favoring "higher types," the modern Mexican power structure aimed to wash clean of Blacks and Indians.

These are some of the Gulf shores of gothic sensibility: between an "impassable gulf" and an "aesthetic eugenics" of passage. From here, we can understand clichéd notions of "Southern soil [...] [as] inherently gothic" (Lloyd 80)—even as we work to stretch perceptions and reading habits further south, and through all of the cardinal points, to see the gothic as well as our shallower modes of multicultural nationalism as a terrified fight-or-flight/flight-or-absorb reaction to possibilities of more dynamic relation. The Gulf of Mexico provides a deep and intimate space (as well as conceptual and performative repertories) for rethinking and moving beyond the supposedly fixed gulf between the living and the (socially) dead that gives gothic its spectral charge. Something in the Gulf region's attentiveness to Days of the Dead, and in its Black Atlantic and Indigenous rapport with death and with the ancestral dead—and something in Gulf peoples' hosting of fabulous genres of boundary-stretching narrative and flexible experience—precedes gothic conventions and unsettles its Euro-settler orientations.

Gothic Gulfs

The Castle of Otranto (1764), that first gothic novel out of a British Empire hitting its colonial and industrial stride, set the script with a haunted castle conveying a sense of omnipresent cultural decadence. Gothic became a mode of representing what is blocked from free movement and aspiration. It harbors what has been pushed back, what we have been inoculated against: something barbaric or monstrous, some undead folklore or occultism untamed by colonial projects. In early US literature—with its savages in the wilderness, racialized anxieties of uprisings, fears of miscegenation, petrification in the face of otherness, hauntings and panics—gothic became a channel for settler-colonial fears surfacing the corruption of supposedly noble regimes. In the hands of those violated by a slaveholding democracy's monstrously normalized acts, gothic also became a mode for "haunting back" as Teresa Goddu has shown (146). Freighted with recognitions of internal monstrosity, gothic grew more directionally southern: a space of quarantines and border walls, paranoia and suppressed memory, doubled consciousness and a deadly performative innocence. Gothic haunts haciendas and constitutions, blows a funk into air we struggle to breathe. It storms with heavy weather, moves with the music of Gulf ports, and carries the voicings of what has been othered, labelled aberrant or queer.

In *Gothic and Modernism: Essaying Dark Literary Modernity* (2008) John Paul Riquelme pointed to how the gothic and modernism intersect in "[t]he crossing of boundaries" and a "refusal of conventional limits" within "a cluster of cultural anxieties to which Gothic writing and literary modernism [...] continue to respond" (7). A certain crossroads modernity, emerging as Riquelme puts it, from "a moment in the history of the British Empire in which extensive contact with other cultures was challenging the hierarchical notion that Europeans were the defining form of humanity," rose from a gothicized "anthropological challenge" (3) presented to and within Euro-modernism. This so-called anthropological challenge points to the limits and failures of gothic, of modernism, and of Western aesthetics and its colonialist perspective. Perhaps this is why a Nobel Prize-winning gothic modernist from Mississippi, William Faulkner, could escape Riquelme's attention. Faulkner wrote from and of a region assumed to be inherently gothic and never quite modern. Even through its many blind spots and gulf impasses, Faulkner's Yoknapatawpha fiction became a touchstone for writers further south and for all sorts of contestation from marginalized perspectives.

Latin American "Boom" writers (1960s–70s, exemplified by Mexico's Carlos Fuentes, Colombia's Gabriel García Márquez, and Peru's Mario Vargas Llosa, among others) responded powerfully to Yoknapatawpha and its narrative entanglements in intensely cross-cultural, racially hierarchical space. Today's generation of Latin American writers and critics—desiring both to affirm strong literary ancestors and to differentiate their handling of the gothic and of magical realism from what Faulkner and the Boom generation bequeathed to them—has been referencing a "tropical gothic," particularly charged in Mexico and Colombia. Gabriel Eljaiek-Rodríguez observes a "tropicalización de lo gótico" in how "the genre is recycled and transformed [...] to enhance the artificiality of the genre and its dynamics of construction and enunciation of the other and to enable the enunciation of the unspeakable" (10). Tropicalization of the gothic draws from many genres and local cultural repertoires in dialogue with Anglo-gothic, including the already tropicalized southern gothic of Poe and Faulkner. Somewhat similarly, works of "Ethno-gothic" or "globalized counter-gothic" as described by critic Arthur Redding (63), strategically engage with gothic conventions in order to *haunt back*, against the grain of a literature "motivated by racial dread" (60). This repurposing of the genre, drawing from Latin American pioneers of a marvelous real, as well as from undead voicings of fable, ritual, and ancestral witness (as in Toni Morrison's *Beloved*), reinhabits a world of gothic hauntings in homeopathic texts of resistance and exorcism (62–63). Our notion of a Gulf gothic includes all of these (re) configurations from across Gulf space and draws from undead repertory excluded from dominant national literary and cultural histories.

Much of what we present in *Gulf Gothic* is a circulation of undead voicings: from the aqueous realm of La Llorona to an uncanny zone of fables and blues fabulation. On Gulf haciendas and plantations, and in port cities from which the goods of colonial conquest and "slavery's capitalism" (as Sven Beckert and Seth Rockman's 2016 collection put it) moved, subalternized peoples and their hard-pressed descendants forced an awareness of their awareness, no matter how shadowy or cutting, on a world built on their backs and land. Much of Gulf writing draws upon a fabulist realm that shares contrapuntal sensibilities with the gothic, the essence of which, as Eric Sundquist has noted, "is the eruption from below of rebellious or unconscious forces and the consequent violation of boundaries, whether racial, sexual, or abstractly moral" (18). Since "Gothic is the means by which the secret history of a culture is told" (Gray 37), and a mode in which "space seems to come alive with agency" (Watson, "So Easy" 3), there is something initiatory and temporally entangled in Gulf gothic performance. We ask what happens when secret histories of the Gulf are told—beyond the usual haunted houses, monsters, madness, and horror—when we look across deeper time and a wider cross-culturality? From days of the dead to carnival and more, Gulf cultures harbor performance repertories of remembering, mourning, initiating, and restoring narrative pharmacopeia.

Gulf Mother, Siren, Specter: La Llorona

Our approach reaches into the distant past and into histories that precede the emergence of the gothic as a genre. What Jay Watson calls gothic's "classic triangular configuration of (1) a monster, a human or nonhuman embodiment of evil; (2) besieged innocence, typically in female form, preferably a young woman endangered sexually; and (3) a haunted castle, preferably dark and mysterious, uncanny in its atmospherics and full of secrets" ("So Easy" 2–3) may be found beyond the gothic—a "beyond" welcomed by the editors of the 2015 collection, *Undead Souths: The Gothic and Beyond in Southern Literature and Culture* (Anderson, Hagood, Turner). For us, the most exemplary gothic character across the Gulf region is one whose presence may be traced across deep measures of time; she is simultaneously a cross-border icon of monstrosity and violated innocence: La Llorona. Classic-era and even pre-Classic Mesoamerican archaeology offers evidence of Llorona-figures coeval with the advent of complexly stratified urban states and the invention of writing. Commonly thought of as originating in post-conquest New Spain, La Llorona's voicings can be discerned from well before European arrival.

In Chapter 1, we attend to the persistence of this siren's presence, from archeological sites in Veracruz to the *Popol Vuh* through the first Mexican horror film—*La Llorona* (1933)—and more recent manifestations. Widely known through tales of a Native woman who was abandoned by her Spanish lover and subsequently drowned their children, she haunts the riverside as a grieving mother/lover and vengeful siren luring incautious children and wayward men. We encounter reroutings of her tales in Sandra Cisneros's "Woman Hollering Creek" and Gloria Anzaldúa's *Borderlands/La Frontera*. We find kinships with a Mesoamerican Llorona in Leslie Marmon Silko's "Yellow Woman" and in narratives by Joy Harjo, LeAnne Howe, and other descendants of Mississippian peoples. We see La Llorona as an undead figure with phantasmal staying power across Gulf time and space. Along with Enrique Ajuria Ibarra, we note "La Llorona's association with flowing water" (132) as a key element of her widely dispersed presence. We depart from Ajuria Ibarra's modern national focus on La Llorona as "a projection of [...] [Mexican] anxieties" and "a repository of transcultural fears" (139) in our reading of her across deeper time and across the Gulf basin. This primal Gulf character cries from boundary waters of the dead, seeking her drowned children and provoking a wide array of fears and desires across haunted borders and texts.

The Split Place: Plantation Settings

The dark castle full of secrets can find its more sublime ancient analogue in Indigenous Chichén Itzá, El Tajín, or Nanih Waiya, but plantation structures provide the most repeated setting of narrative haunted by the afterlives of conquest and the Atlantic slave trade along the Gulf. In no writer is this gothic sense for the region's unspeakable trauma more widely recognized than in William Faulkner's creation of Yoknapatawpha County, Mississippi. Jace Weaver has identified Yoknapatawpha as "a compound of the Choctaw/Chickasaw words 'yocona' and 'petopha,' earth and split," making its "split earth" a marker and metaphor for multiple splittings: of Indigenous people from their land, and of people from each other and from the land itself ("Splitting the Earth" 66–67). Yoknapatawpha becomes scene of the crime, representative space of "psychic homocide" (*That the People Might Live*, 38). Choctaw writer LeAnne Howe notes the appropriative turnings of Faulkner's self-proclaimed "little postage stamp of native soil" and how he "took the Chickasaw place name of a home he and his ancestors were familiar with [Yakni Patafa] and used it in his fiction" ("Faulkner Didn't Invent Yoknapatawpha" 5). Yoknapatawpha's "split earth"—as plantation space of Native removal and of slavery's capitalism—provides uncanny counterpoint (a kind of monstrous double) to the sacred account of human origins articulated in the *Popol Vuh*: "Split Place, Bitter Water Place is the name: the yellow corn, white corn came from there" (Tedlock 145), that is, "Paxil [...] 'broken, split, or cleft'" place (Christenson 179). Articulated in modernist prose and recognized by Mexican writers such as Juan Rulfo, Carlos Fuentes, and Sergio Pitol for its cross-pollenizations and resemblances to hacienda systems of land-holding, labor, and production, Yoknapatawpha and its gothic modernism circulated further south, as Deborah Cohn, among others, has shown.

In Chapter 2, we examine the plantation setting of *Gulf Gothic*, drawing upon the modern history of the region and its folk forms of contrapuntal witness such as the fable and Gulf music. We look to Vicente Riva Palacio's "The Thirty-three *Negros*" (1870) for its treatment of events surrounding Crown concessions to an African maroon community led by Yanga in colonial Veracruz (1609), as well as works in the fugitive slave-narrative tradition—read as gothicized initiation tales traversing supposedly impassable gulfs. We focus primarily, however, on two novels of initiatory horror: one by Faulkner and another by Carlos Fuentes published within two decades of each other. Faulkner's *Go Down, Moses* (1942) presents a shifting plantation frontier over at least 150 years. Initiations into secret histories (and haunting Gulf knowledge) are multiple, taking place in hunting camps, in readings of the plantation ledger, in connections to the port of New Orleans and the wider world, through contestatory witness and a legacy of sacrificed lives and disavowed relations. We follow Faulkner's already tropicalized southern gothicism further south through its imprint on Fuentes's *The Death of Artemio Cruz* (1962). A novel of the Mexican Revolution's betrayal of its ideals, *La muerte de Artemio Cruz* houses the deathbed consciousness of the protagonist and the secrets of Cocuya—the Veracruz hacienda of his lowly birth and adult reclamation. Cruz, who became the monstrous boss whom the revolution aimed to overthrow, is revealed as the man of African descent whom modern Mexico strived to erase through ideologies of *mestizaje*. There is nothing new about presenting the plantation or hacienda as gothic setting built on racialized structures of impasse. However, the gothicized split-places, evasions, and complicities of Yoknapatawpha and Cocuya—read in relation through the ports of New Orleans and Veracruz (key ports of the Atlantic slave trade), draw out a fetidness in the entrails of global modernity—a wider gulf's bad air and bad faith that never quite pass.

Climate: Huracán

Southern gothic, for critic Richard Gray, may boil down to mega weather, a "[s]low, brooding intensity building up to a moment of storm" and atmospherics so charged that "if there is a deep central rhythm at work in the South, and so lurking there in works from and about the region, it is that" (26). For him, this "regional rhythm"—thick with "the weather of the landscape and the weather of the mind"—tracks so fully into "the rhythm of the Gothic" (26) that "'Southern Gothic' seems almost a tautology" (27). But how so? Has the gothic taken such a deep southern dive as a genre that it has been tropicalized in its postplantation transculturations? Or is it that the regionalization of the US (or global) south comes with gothic border walls formed to hold a nation's heat, decadence, and bad air at bay? Readers can find such weather further south and centuries earlier in the presence of Huracán in Maya and Popoluca creation accounts, as well as in *The Book of Chilam Balam of Chumayel*. A colonial-era Maya textual assemblage, *The Chilam Balam* presents a history of storms in the Yucatan peninsula from before Spanish conquest to the "Blood vomit" and "Famine" that reigned until Chac ykal (Hurricane) killed Father Agustín Gómez in the year 1661 (Edmonson 223). Since weather has no respect for national borders, Mexican and Gulf gothic may also be tautological. Or rather, seemingly self-evident categories and frontiers may shore up false innocence and exceptionalist identifications.

"[W]eather of the landscape and the weather of the mind," if this is southern gothic, then we must redraw the maps to engage larger tropical systems that feed into Gulf landscapes and thought. Zora Neale Hurston's *Their Eyes Were Watching God*, Eudora Welty's "The Winds," Linda Hogan's *Power*, Kate Chopin's "The Storm," and Lydia Cabrera's *Afro-Cuban Tales* all work with Huracán's Mesoamerican and Arawak narrative core as well as with West African rhythms of weather sweeping across a heated Atlantic. Hurricanes begin as tropical patterns associated with the Yoruba deity Oya and the Mande Buffalo-woman (whirlwinds, water buffalo avatars, and death rites), gathering force off the Senegambian coast. Divination presents Oya as libidinal whirlwind and cosmic house-cleaner clearing up repressed, climatically imbalanced conditions: "Swept-clean means Oya" (Gleason 44). If we take Gulf atmospherics seriously, the whole sweep of the Anthropocene enters the picture, from the *Popol Vuh* to the plantation-era arrival of Oya's batá drums and Shakespeare's "Tempest." The Gulf hosts a cosmic Llorona who moves across generic, national, and linguistic borderwaters [...] beyond gothic.

Chapter 3 addresses atmospheric storm-pressures driving two Gulf novels of our times: Jesmyn Ward's *Salvage the Bones* (2011) from coastal

Mississippi in the wake of Hurricane Katrina, and Fernanda Melchor's *Temporada de huracanes* (2017) from coastal Veracruz, translated as the Booker Prize-finalist *Hurricane Season* (2020). Both create fictional worlds impacted by Yoknapatawpha (Ward's Bois Sauvage and Melchor's La Matosa), and both draw on a mythic storm presence run amuck. Ward's *Salvage the Bones* begins with a pit bull birthing puppies, a TV station tracking Hurricane Katrina, and allusions to Faulkner and Greek myths of the infanticidal Medea (a canonical Llorona). Fifteen-year-old Esch Batiste, pregnant, faces Hurricane Katrina with her family in long-brewing conditions of structural violence. The storm is a force of gothic knowledge, apocalyptic and transformative [...] exposing a gutted or gutless state. From further south in Veracruz, Melchor's *Hurricane Season* also addresses Gulf mega-weather. Sentences swirl for pages without punctuation. Four narrative points of view wrap around the growing storm's communal eye: the murder of a contemporary Witch. Four cardinal points by which the rains have long been invoked structure this crime story spilling the postplantation Gulf's violent open secrets: femicide, sexual abuse, homophobia, corruption, poverty, addiction, race-and-class struggle, and all the suffering wrought by narco and oil economies fueling neoliberal consumerism. The steady atmospherics of storm draw readers' attention to the characters' proneness to storm conditions and their/our entanglement in a political economy in which the "Visceraless State", as Cristina Rivera Garza observes, turns "its back on its obligations and responsibilities, surrendering before the unrelenting, lethal logic of profit" (4). The gutted, gutless state—whether Mississippi or Veracruz, the US or Mexico—is one we painfully recognize in Ward's Bois Sauvage and Melchor's La Matosa, its impasses and climate of violence supercharged by a Gulf that "is daily widening."

Even the most cursory notion of a *"Cornbread Nation"* (as advanced in an annual collection of *"The Best of Southern Food Writing"* from the University of Mississippi-based Southern Foodways Alliance) owes enormous debts not only to Mississippian First Nations but also to Mesoamerican maize cultures of monumental mound-building, ball games, feathered serpent iconography, and salutes to the four directions that impacted Puebloan peoples along the upper Rio Grande and Mississippian cultures from Spiro (Oklahoma) and Moundville (Alabama) to Cahokia (Illinois) as Michael Blake, Susan Power, and Karl Taub have observed. An ancient Gulf culture exists. A postplantation/postcolonial Gulf culture holds staying power as well along widening fissures that shape our nations and the larger world, all impacted by Atlantic storm systems that move across Gulf waters with increasingly overwhelming force. Gothic has been a key mode of surfacing what has been excluded from consciousness even as it has tended to repeat old patterns of displacing its monsters, its ghosts and specters. We seek an accounting here. One of us, a scholar of Latin American and Mexican literatures and cultures, born and raised in the Gulf state of Veracruz; and the other a scholar of the US south and the African Diaspora, working from the Florida coast. Our notion of a Gulf gothic or set of gothic gulfs includes southern gothic, a Mexican *gótico tropical*, and much that exceeds, tropes upon, and precedes any notion of the gothic—including fables, initiation tales, divination narratives, folk songs and YouTube videos, and the power-shows of ancient Mesoamerican stelae. In a world of widening gulfs, we seek to engage gulfs between us [...] in a manner that has long been the terrain of the gothic undead.

Chapter 1

LA LLORONA'S UNDEAD VOICES: WOMAN AT THE BORDERWATERS

Ay, de mí Llorona, Llorona, Llorona
Llévame al río [...]

> "La Llorona," as sung by Ángela Aguilar

There's always / something left to lose.

> Deborah Miranda, "The Zen of La Llorona"

If a single character links cinematic horror and gothic narrative with the deep time of the Gulf, it is La Llorona, rising from haunting boundary waters. She moves, like the gothic itself, from nightmare and uncertain boundaries, and is simultaneously the imperiled young protagonist and monstrous siren, wronged, infanticidal, and vengeful. Mothers tell her tale to keep children from wandering after dark, and away from rivers or creeks where they can be swept into the spirit realm. But her provocations are also recounted within earshot of potentially wayward romantic partners. She is a fatal attraction spoken of by those who live to tell of her—beautiful and ominous, Indigenous and mestiza, her wailing voice associated with water, eros welled up inside.

Imagine growing up along the Rio Blanco in Ciudad Mendoza, a small town in the mountains of central Veracruz, where everyone can tell a version of the tale. A Náhuatl-speaker from La Cuesta—a pueblo up the mountain from Mendoza—speaks of a weeping woman who appears in a long white dress on the river's shores, seducing roving men. Men drawn to La Llorona are often left psychically shattered or found dead from heart attack. These tales caution boyfriends and husbands to stay faithful, while reminding women of the vigilance necessary to protecting their households. People across Veracruz know La Llorona's backstory and the horrifying remorse of her action: the drowning of her children following her Spanish (or elite criollo) partner's abandonment of her for a more class-appropriate woman. Her subsequent suicide. With no place in Heaven, she wanders between Limbo and Earth, seeking her children's souls in the waters, bringing grief to men to whom she remains both attracted and repulsed.

Higher in the mountains, by the Sierra Madre headwaters of the Rio Blanco, a classic-era stone monolith found near the cloud-swept town of Maltrata bears witness to an early example of an American woman's literary voice (AD 600–900). This "Lady of Maltrata," as Cherra Wyllie writes, "emits a speech scroll" much like the comic book caption of a superhero ("In Search," 171). Wearing a royal headdress, she speaks to an attendant in a scene annotated with glyphic, numbered day signs. Although what she says is no longer legible, her voicing testifies to her agency. The Lady of Maltrata points us to a "Gulf Coast tradition of elite women [...] engaged in religious ritual related to political affairs" (168), and her authority "recall[s] the most famous of all Gulf Coast women: Doña Maria (Malintzin or Malinche), a key actor in the Spanish Conquest" (172).

No Mexican can forget Malinche, the Náhuatl-speaking woman from the south of Veracruz who served as Cortés' "tongue," his translator-guide and lover. Malinche was abandoned first by her parents and then—when she was no longer crucial to the conquest—by Cortés (father of her son), who married her off to one of his officers in Orizaba, on the banks of the Rio Blanco. Malinche is often swept into Llorona tales blaming her as traitor to the Mexica (Aztec) state, making her infanticidal and pitiful, *la chingada*—the fucked mother, "the Mother forcibly opened, violated or deceived" (79)—of modern Mexico, one of the "self-engendered phantasms" of a past carried "within us" (72–73), "a mythical figure [...] like *La Llorona*" (75), as Octavio Paz influentially presented her. The misogyny associated with these tales fixes Malinche as symbol of conquest and violation, of ambivalence over the nation's racialized origins. But Llorona's presence in Mesoamerica, we argue, is much older than Malinche.

If we follow the Rio Blanco from the mountains of central Veracruz to the Gulf, we come to Classic-era ruins at El Zapotal (AD 600–900) and the shrine of the skeletal Death God: a large "masterwork of unbaked clay" holding court from a pyramidal platform and surrounded by U-shaped mural-adorned walls on the mounded site (Wyllie, "The mural paintings" 211). Here, in 1971, Manuel Torres Guzmán excavated nineteen life-sized terracotta female figures that had been arranged in procession alongside the Death God. These *cihuateteo*—as Sara Ladrón de Guevara describes them, are figures of women who died in childbirth, "considered goddesses [...] equated with the hierarchy of warriors killed in battle" (90). Each is individuated, with eyes closed, mouths open in wailing or song, the upper bodies nude, clothed in skirts from waist to feet. A belt ends in "two snake heads hanging over the skirt [...] linked to fertility [...] also associated with death" (93). The *cihuateteo* accompany the setting sun into the underworld to assist its birth at dawn. Their exquisitely crafted terracotta figures wailed from mounded underworlds by the Rio Blanco at its Gulf mouth. And now, in a museum in the state capitol of Xalapa, their silent cries bear witness to Llorona's classic-era prefigurations.

What could be more gothic than a death-shrine to the Lord of the Underworld enclosing nineteen wailing attendants who died in childbirth? Except that it is from here that the sun rises, and it is from the sprouting maize symbol crowning this skeletal Lord that the kingdom is fed. Since Mesoamericans have awareness of several world creations and destructions across time, little here fits into a European gothic's doomsday clock. This is something else. In the Rio Blanco towns of Nogales and Orizaba in central Veracruz, inhabitants speak of siren-inhabited springs from which a *sirena* offers a treasure to the man who can carry her from the waters to the church altar without once looking back as she shifts shape and wails. The man who can walk with the feminine in the totality of its forms and not be petrified by what he might call monstrous is the rarest of suitor-survivors. Along the Gulf and the rivers that feed it, a multi-form Llorona grieves and calls in her thin homespun white dress. She is the region's widespread siren figure: its undead embodiment of longing.

Many Lloronas: From Xtaj and Xpuch to Sixth Omen and Cinematic Gothic

Something of La Llorona inhabits the *Popol Vuh*, rendered in K'iche' Maya through the Roman alphabet between the 1550s and 1560s. Michael D. Coe pioneered the search for continuities between *Popol Vuh* narratives and classic-era representations in Maya ceramics, stelae, and surviving books of glyphic writing. More recently, Oswaldo Chinchilla Mazariegos found several motifs from the *Popol Vuh* to be "nodal subjects" repeated in a long continuum of Mesoamerican mythology. We read La Llorona's presence in this way in the *Popol Vuh* (through various translations into Spanish and English). A group of elders, terrified by abductions and sacrifices of their people to K'iche' deities, plots to entrap these divinities who appear as "spirit boys" bathing in local streams. As Tedlock presents it, the elders find two "choice maidens who radiate preciousness" and give them their mission:

> You must go, our dear daughters. Go wash clothes at the river, and if you should see three boys, undress yourselves in front of them. And if their hearts should desire you, you will titillate them. [...] Then they should give you something. If they like your faces you must really give yourselves up to them. And if you do not give yourselves up, then we shall kill you. We'll feel satisfied when you bring back a sign, since we'll think of it as proof that they came after you. (167)

The daughters sent to the river are Xtaj and Xpuch, "Lust Woman" and "Wailing Woman" (167, 310) or "Lady Lust and Lady Wailing" (Christenson 225). They go to "be violated by the spirit familiars" of the K'iche' deities, but the boy-*naguals* show discerning restraint (Tedlock 168). They question the maidens, discovering their task and providing them with "signs of their sin" (169): cloaks imprinted with the K'iche' beings' "threefold inscription"— jaguar, eagle, and wasp signs (168). When the girls bring these cloaks back home, the wasp-inscribed cloak unleashes a stinging swarm on the community, for which the two women are blamed: "the tribes continued to think of them as temptresses" (169). Recinos presents them as "sirens" (197) sent to the river to "become whores" (199). The scapegoating of Llorona-figures probably did not begin with Spanish conquest. Something older, already present, placed Xtaj and Xpuch in these roles.

Chinchilla Mazariegos finds "multiple analogues" in classic, colonial, and contemporary Mesoamerican representation "in which amorous seduction led to the defeat and demise of mythical heroes" (198). He observes that "Aquatic settings with water lilies, fish, and other aquatic creatures are common in classic representations of the Maize god's affairs with women" (201). The stream where Xtaj and Xpuch go to meet the K'iche' deities marks a repeating locus of carnal knowledge, disaster, and conquest as well as fertility. The K'iche' deities' forebears are the Maya hero twins who played ball with guardians of the underworld and died there, but had their ashes mixed with cornmeal and tossed in a river. They emerged as catfishboys ready for new ballgames and shapeshiftings (190–91). Cornbread catfishboys from spiritworlds, Lust Woman and Wailing Woman, this is the stuff of maize culture's undead voicings.

Many acounts of La Llorona trace her to an omen recorded in Fray Bernardino de Sahagún's compilation and translation of Aztec accounts of the conquest. His *Historia general de las cosas de la Nueva España* (*The Florentine Codex*, Book 8) presents "the sixth omen" of impending doom as "a woman [çihoatl], who went weeping and crying out at night," saying "O my beloved sons, now we are at the point of going!" (18). Illustrated with a snake's body, a woman's head, and hair shaped in a pair of horns, she is the first of the feminine Mexica deities described in Book One of Sahagún's seminal work of Western anthropology. Cihuacoatl appears as "an evil omen to men; she brought men misery," was "covered with chalk" and "garbed in white" for nocturnal wanderings, "weeping, wailing" (11). She bears affinity to a maize-goddess, Chicome coatl or "Seven Snake" (13) and to a water-deity, Chalchiuhtli ycue, feared for her tendency to drown whoever enters her waters (21). As Domino Renee Perez notes, "Motecuçoma believed the goddess Cihuacoatl […] to be the likely source of the wailing," arguing that testimony of her as the Sixth Omen "represents the first documented recounting of La Llorona" (17).

One of the functions of gothic narrative has been the exposure and release of repressed truth. Xtaj's Aztec equivalent was Tlazoltéotl, "Eater-of-Filth." Beverido Duhalt writes of the contrasts in this deity's representation along the Gulf, and how in central Veracruz, Tlazoltéotl has "a black mouth, which alludes to her role as devourer of filth, the goddess who eats what human beings are purged of. However, in Huasteca representations what stands out is her power of seduction, her sensuality and her link with the phases of the Moon" (75). Sahagún devoted pages to Tlazoltéotl in Book One of his *General History of the Things of New Spain,* noting how she offered a once-in-a-lifetime opportunity of confession: "one spread before her all unclean works—however ugly, however grave; avoiding nothing because of shame," and subsequently "[s]he cleansed one; she washed one" (23). When such a system is functional, what is the need of gothic? Contemporary gothic provides a key means of spreading out the unclean works of postcolonial Gulf experience for acknowledgment, recognition, and prescriptive treatment. We trace La Llorona's emergence from Xtaj and Xpuch, Cihuacoatl and Tlazoltéotl, and other nodal variants that shifted shape after the conquest, transforming yet again across Mexico from 1848 to 1933 in confluence with a surge of international gothic expression.

With the 1933 film, *La Llorona,* Mexico embraced the cinematic world of gothic horror. Two years earlier, Hollywood classics such as *Dracula, Frankenstein* and *Dr. Jekyl and Mr Hyde* (1931) had drawn on the genre's typical settings: a medieval castle in Transylvania, an estate in the Bavarian Alps, a dark house in Victorian London. With *La Llorona,* cinematic gothic was Americanized. Before the film's production, Hollywood horror had played in Mexico but had not been made in Mexico for Mexican audiences. Cuban director Ramón Peón turned to a labyrinthine dark house and a five-act theatrical structure to narrate two strands of Llorona legend. The film opens in a twentieth-century world: a man dying from a heart attack to the sound of a woman's wailing, cutting to his corpse in a hospital morgue, the urbane Dr. Ricardo de Acuña presiding. The next cut moves to the fourth birthday party of the doctor's son, and a festive mood turns to ominous discussion in the library, with the doctor's father-in-law Don Fernando calling for caution—explaining how his brother had died mysteriously upon turning four. When Don Fernando pulls a volume from the shelf and reads, the scene fades to a spacious sixteenth-century home.

Here, the audience meets Doña Ana Xicotécatl, lover of Don Rodrigo de Cortés and mother of his child. When this Cortés descendant betrays Ana to wed a woman of his own rank and race, Ana crashes the wedding and then returns home to kill her son and finally herself with an obsidian knife (her Aztec ring flashing), and her ghost rises in spectral wailing.

Back in the modern library of what could be the same updated colonial home, Dr. de Acuña interrupts the reading: "That's just the legend of La Llorona [...]!" When the dismissive doctor rejoins his wife and child, a hooded intruder who had been listening through a keyhole raises an obsidian knife (and familiar Aztec ring) to the dramatic sound of drums, and a wail rises off-screen, leaving the grandfather murdered while the intruder slips into labyrinthine passages to abduct the birthday boy, dropping him finally in retreat to a dungeon-like basement. Once summoned, the police enter the basement where they discover a second book hidden beneath a floor panel—revealing a curse on the family as well as the curse's source in Cortés and Malinche.

With this second book, emphatic drumming moves to a flashback scene where Malinche is abandoned and Cortés takes their four-year-old son. Traumatized and murmuring—"my son, my son"—Malinche tries pitifully to steal another's child, before killing herself with the obsidian knife, her ring glinting on her hand. Backed by the soundtrack's drumming, Malinche's maid takes knife and ring from her lady's corpse, vowing eternal revenge on the first-born son of Cortés's lineage as a wailing ghost rises in response. Suddenly we are back on the Doctor's basement steps, the detective concluding his reading. The cellar door slams shut, the mother wails, and the hooded intruder pulls the birthday-boy through a passage behind a bookshelf. As police give chase into the basement, the kidnapper lays the child beneath a large Coatlicue statue hidden over centuries. A zoom-shot lingers on the ring on the knife-wielding hand against the wall's stacked-skull backdrop, followed by shots as the dark figure collapses, and the boy is saved. With the hooded intruder's face finally revealed, we recognize the family's maid. La Llorona rises in ghostly white from the servant's body [...] into the Coatlicue statue at film's end.

This film marks the arrival of Mexican gothic, indigenized but not Indigenous. Drums and hidden texts, Coatlicue's haunting basement presence in a mansion once owned by Cortés, give *La Llorona* its gothic turns carried by the family servant. In each household of the Mexican elite, the film seems to say, even among audiences of Hispano-criollo pretensions, "the help" lurks in ominous alliance with undead forces. *La Llorona* rises from American antiquity, but takes its gothic formations from the nation's postcolonial anxieties. The initial 1933 *La Llorona* speaks to tensions behind domestic relationships across the Gulf, evoked increasingly in recent film, from *The Help* (2011) with its infamous shit-laced chocolate pie, to *Roma* (2018) featuring an Indigenous servant who saves her child-charge from drowning on a Gulf beach, to a powerful Guatemalan *La Llorona* (2019) in which a retired dictator's undead Maya servant holds the family—and nation—accountable for genocide.

The text pulled from the basement of the 1933 film could well be José Maria Marroqui's *La Llorona: cuento histórico mexicano* (1887). Marroqui's Llorona introduces herself: "I am Malitzin, whom the vulgar Spaniards called Malinche" (25), and recounts how she was given to a Lord of Tabasco, then offered in tribute to Cortés, who seduced her and had her serve as interpreter and counselor. Abandoned by Cortés, she dies in remorse for her treason in becoming "one of the most effective tools of the conquest" (89). At Malitzin's death an angel assigns penance of three centuries of sleep by day in Lake Texcoco, with nights spent "walking the city in tears [...] inflicting terror on the residents" (95), all for crime against "the first duty that the homeland imposes on its children, far from defending it, you betrayed it" (92). Publishing his tale in the modernized Mexico City of the Porfirio Díaz regime, Marroqui recounts a past that has passed [...] even if its colonial anxieties remain. The Porfiriato with its specter-dispelling electric lights, railways, factories, and telegraph systems, announces an era free of Lloronas while conveying the lesson of a treasonous Malinche, all under a thirty-four year dictatorship that was selling the nation's resources to the highest bidder. This is the work of a criollo gothic on the verge of the Revolution of 1910 and its remaking of the nation from below.

Early nationalist gothic worked hard to dismiss an Indigenous presence that haunted it. *La Llorona's* criollo antecedents appear in Mexico's first historical novel: *La hija del judío*, published in installments in *El Fénix de Campeche* from 1848 to 1851 by Yucatec writer Justo Sierra O'Reilly. Set in Mérida during the Holy Inquisition two centuries earlier, *La hija del judío* [*The Jew's Daughter*] follows Walter Scott's narrative style, presenting a young heroine stalked by representatives of the Inquisition and colonial government. In the novel's storylines of forbidden love, colonial crime, and Jesuit power struggles, Ana Mitlich Osuna sees early national fiction turning to the gothic, "configuring colonial space as oppressive space, asphyxiating and maleficent" (9), while managing to exclude Mexico's Indigenous population, as well as Africans enslaved within the system. This gothic construction of a Mexican criollo imaginary holds much in common with the rise of national (and southern) identities in the United States. Also submerged beneath the borders of national histories is the fact that Sierra O'Reilly began writing *La hija del judío* in Washington, DC in 1847 as he was seeking US intervention in the Maya uprising in Yucatán. Maya forces had reclaimed much of their territory and were marching on Mérida in what came to be called the Caste War, with an Indigenous Maya state maintaining independence from 1847 to 1901. As Claudio Palomares Salas observes, Sierra O'Reilly rewrote Mérida's colonial past "to provide a foundational text for the ephemeral Republic of Yucatán" (1841–48), the southern sister of the Lone Star Republic of Texas (1836–46), while he was offering Yucatán's annexation to the US in return for military aid against the Maya. Had Mexico not intervened first, the entire peninsula could have been admitted into the United States for the protection of Euro-criollo landowners and power. Sierra O'Reilly's novel ignores the region's Indigenous population, using "the Spanish Jew" as a cipher to "reinterpret the peninsula's history in order to create a national utopia that excluded Jews" (215), that is, Mayas.

Centuries of repressive exclusion and violence add urgency to contemporary Maya writing. The Maya sirena-seductress, the X-táabay, appears in tales by Doroteo Chan Briceño from Chumayel in a collection of Yucatec Maya narrative (2007). Chan Briceño insists, "the X-táabay exists" (58, 70) and walks Maya lands. One tale recalls a nephew who was nearly carried away while playing cards with friends in the moonlight; he escapes after questioning the X-táabay's gestures to him: *"Who could this woman be who walks out so late in the night?"* (70). Doroteo Chan Briceño's cautionary tales mark gendered boundaries of appropriate behavior. Men, however, often push back, as does the collection's editor, Feliciano Sánchez Chan, in one of his poems in Yucatec Maya titled "Xko' óolal Xtáabay" ("Seductress Xtáabay"):

Tie me, entangle me, strangle me,
take me to your mystery
seductress Xtáabay
where life doesn't matter
or hell either
if your paradise is enough. (99)

Captivated by "the gulfs of your eyes" (99), Sánchez Chan embraces his entanglement with this Yucatec muse/seductress while working steadily to shore up literacy in the mother tongue.

No source conveys La Llorona's haunting of a Mexican poetics of yearning and loss quite like the folk song enthralled by her memory. Flora Botton-Burlá compiled 121 strophes of "La Llorona" gathered from a performative repertory in constant variation. The earliest date she gives for a print version is 1932, with the song's source located in the Isthmus of Tehuantepec (Oaxaca and southern Veracruz). Miguel Covarrubias's *Mexico South* (1947) introduced "La Llorona" to a US audience (329–30), invoking a woman of captivating beauty recalled along a southern river's shores. Like wailing blues figures on the Mississippi, La Llorona is simultaneously localized and national or international. Among recent YouTube videos are examples from the regional core (a version by Lila Downs from Oaxaca, and another from Veracruz's Natalia LaFourcade) along with a stunningly plaintive performance in which sixteen-year-old Los Angeles-based Ángela Aguilar sings of a girl becoming Llorona in the dazzling face-paint of a Day of the Dead market: an ofrenda of beyond-gothic glamour and renewed liminal spirit.

We have outlined the rise of a Mexican gothic in key moments from Sierra O'Reilly's *La hija del judio* (1848–51) to Marroqui's *La Llorona* (1887), Péon's 1933 horror film of the same name, and Ángela Aguilar's video-version of the classic folksong (2018). It has become standard to ground the Llorona legend in tales of Cortés's betrayal of Malinche and her alleged betrayal of Indigenous America, as well as in Montezuma's paralysis in the face of the goddess Cihuacoatl's night-wailing (read as sixth omen of the Mexicas' impending downfall). La Llorona comes to us as a figure of apocalyptic postcolonial anxieties. We believe, however, that proto-Llorona siren-figures were prevalent across the southern Gulf region from deep into the Mesoamerican classic period. From Maya sirens to Veracruz cihuateteo accompanying the Lord of Death on the banks of the Rio Blanco, we find proto-Llorona wailing figures and siren-seductresses moving in a fabulous domain—akin to what "gothic" would become—in an enduring Gulf folk culture. These Lloronas had already traversed the Rio Grande with the spread of maize culture before any European "discovered" or "betrayed" them.

"The Same Web of Survival": From Woman Hollering Creek to Yellow Woman

Across our borderwaters, La Llorona has emerged as an icon of Mexican American and Chicana feminism. Clarissa Pinkola Estés recounts how a young woman was seduced by a businessman along the Rio Grande. Pregnant, she drank water contaminated by her lover's factories, and her twins "were born blind and with webbed fingers" (302). This resistant Llorona haunts the riverside, grieving for what has been poisoned and drowned, voicing her cry in *"temblón,* shiver stories" (Pinkola Estes 302). Gloria Anzaldúa, in *Borderlands/La Frontera* (1987), affirmed the critical witness implicit in La Llorona's solitary cry (33), presenting her—along with the Virgin of Guadeloupe and Malinche—as one of the three mothers of *"La gente Chicana"* and "a combination of the other two" (30). Anzaldúa, from the south Texas Gulf-border, proceeded in her later work to present La Llorona as a healer or *nepantlera,* native to the "nepantla," "a Náhuatl word for an in-between state" (*The Gloria Anzaldúa Reader* 180), a figure of both border and gulf. According to Anzaldúa, nepantleras "help us make the crossings, and guide us through the transformation process" (310) to a kind of Gulf-knowledge or "double being-ness" (277). In alignment with Anzaldúa and Pinkola Estés, José Límon's folkloric studies also recognized La Llorona as a "potent symbol of resistance" (410) key to "Mexican women's symbolic repertoire for responding to domination" (419). For Límon, La Llorona's tears and omnipresent river provide an aqueous realm where her children may be reborn.

Sandra Cisneros was among the early wave of Chicana writers embracing La Llorona. Her story "Woman Hollering Creek" (1991) is the most widely read engagement with Llorona-lore in American fiction. Here, she flips the gothic script of a besieged victim and infanticidal mother and moves her protagonist and child away from drownings. We read what it means for a woman to cross borders between Mexico and the US, between Spanish and English [...] into a Texas community that cannot explain the meaning or origin of the name of the creek running through town: "*Pues, allá de los indios, quién sabe*" (46). The text, however, knows the answer, guiding its protagonist Cleófilas, who, having followed her husband "to a town *en el otro lado*" (43), finds herself sitting by the creekbank in despair with her young son.

Cisneros's story moves its weeping woman to become a joyously hollering protagonist. The name of Woman Hollering Creek translates into Spanish as "La Gritona": "Such a funny name for such a lovely *arroyo*," Cleófilas wonders as she coinsiders "whether the woman had hollered from anger or pain" (46). Increasingly abused and ignored by her husband, she finds companionship with "the neighbor ladies" by her creekside house: Soledad and Dolores, both women unable to forget "the men who had left through either choice or circumstance" (47). Soledad (Solitude) with her telenovelas, and Dolores (Sorrows or Pain) tending her "red flowers," "a thick menstrual color" (47), surround Cleófilas with the condition of La Llorona. On good nights Cleófilas accompanies her husband to the ice house, where the men drink and talk and "she sits mute" (48). The men swap words over beers, "trying to find the truth lying at the bottom of the bottle like a gold dubloon on the sea floor" (48). As the men drink, "what is bumping like a helium balloon at the ceiling of the brain never finds its way out," and they drown inside themselves in rage: "the fists try to speak" (48). To make matters worse, this side of the border has been "built so that you have to depend on husbands" (50–51); there is nothing within walking distance and "no place to go" except to "the neighbor ladies," Soledad on one side, Dolores on the other. Or to Woman Hollering Creek: "a thing with a voice all its own, all day and all night calling" (51). Sitting creekside with her son, pregnant and alienated, Cleófilas asks, "Is it La Llorona, the weeping woman? La Llorona, who drowned her children?" (51).

In the telenovelas that guide Cleófilas' understanding, violence against women is normalized and pervasive. Once her husband's abusive behavior builds, Cleófilas begins to see femicidal patterns: the newspapers "full of such stories. This woman found on the side of the interstate. This one pushed from a moving car. This one's cadaver, this one unconscious, this one beaten blue" (52). However, the pattern is disrupted when, after a series of beatings, she insists on going to the clinic for a prenatal check. There, Graciela (Grace), who conducts the ultrasound and sees the bruises, and Graciela's friend Felice (Happiness) intervene to change the narrative from its gothic tracks. Felice shows up in her pickup truck to drive Cleófilas and her son to catch a bus across the border. On the bridge crossing the creek past town, Felice "opened her mouth and let out a yell as loud as any mariachi" (55). Back in her father's home in Mexico, Cleófilas recalls this moment: "Who would've thought? [...] Pain or rage, perhaps, but not a hoot" like Felice's (56). As Cleófilas narrates, her voice flows: "gurgling out of her own throat, a long ribbon of laughter, like water" (56). For critic Claire Joysmith these crossings "are transformed into nepantla in-between spaces," Anzaldúa's "liminal-space between the way things had been and an unknown future."

We view La Llorona herself as a nepantlera of Gulf crossings and transitions. We know that the Mexicas migrated southward from Azatlán and that the Comanche language shares linguistic roots with Náhuatl. We also know that maize culture moved northward from Olmec trade routes and from south-central Mexico up the Rio Grande along with trade items such as cacao and quetzal feathers. An exemplary modern text tapping into this cultural matrix linking the New Mexican headwaters of the Rio Grande with sources such as the Maya *Popol Vuh* is Leslie Marmon Silko's *Storyteller* (1981).

The story "Yellow Woman," from the collection *Storyteller* by Laguna Pueblo writer Leslie Marmon Silko, draws from a four-directional maize-ceremonial complex kin to the one through which "Thunder Woman, Yellow Woman / Cacao Woman and Cornmeal Woman" are evoked in the *Popol Vuh* (Tedlock 103). Silko's "Yellow Woman" opens to a riverbank erotics: "My thigh clung to his with dampness. [...] I could hear the water, almost at our feet where the narrow fast channel bubbled" (54). The narrator feels caught between gulf-matrices of time, identity, and narrative, trying to assert her everyday identity both to herself and to this man with whom she has slept by the river:

[...] I only said that you were him and that I was Yellow Woman—I'm not really her—I have my own name and I come from the pueblo on the other side of the mesa. Your name is Silva and you are a stranger I met by the river yesterday afternoon. (55)

She insists, "the old stories about the ka'tsina spirit and Yellow Woman can't mean us" (55). But since Yellow Woman narrates the traditional stories in which she is abducted by a wild spirit, our narrator begins "wondering if Yellow Woman had known who she was—if she knew that she would become part of the stories" (55). She summons resistance to a script of spirit-possession: "I am not Yellow Woman. Because she is from out of time past and I live now and I've been to school and there are highways and pickup trucks that Yellow Woman never saw" (56). Such reasoning proves weak, however, as she rides by horseback to Silva's lava-rock mountain home. Our narrator reasserts, "'I don't believe it. Those stories couldn't happen now'" (57), to which Silva/ka'tsina-spirit responds, "But someday they will talk about us, and they will say, 'Those two lived long ago when things like that happened" (57).

From atop the mesa, Silva surveys four cultural-linguistic directions: the Navajo reservation, Pueblo lands, Texan ranches, and Mexican vaquero communities. He undresses his captive, and she pulls away: "He pulled me around and pinned me down with his arms and chest. 'You don't understand, do you, little Yellow Woman? You will do what I want'" (58). Silva, however, as mountain spirit, is no gothic monster, and Yellow Woman is not bereft of agency, even as "I lay underneath him and I knew that he could destroy me" (58). What she gains in the encounter is "the kind of feeling for him that overcame me that morning along the river" (58), an erotic gnosis rooted in an epistemology worlds away from European gothic. She imagines her mother, grandmother, husband, and child wondering over her absence, the tribal police searching for her, and she knows "there will be a story about the day I disappeared while I was walking along the river," and knows what her grandfather would say: "Stolen by a ka'tsina, a mountain spirit. She'll come home—they usually do" (59).

The clear potential for femicide is here, but "Yellow Woman" follows a different script. After Silva butchers "a beef carcass" from a rustling foray in the valley, the two ride towards a community of Mexicans to sell the meat. A white cowboy intercepts the pair, accuses them of rustling his cattle, and Yellow Woman knows Silva's approaching thunderstorm: "something I could feel in my stomach—in his eyes, and when I glanced at his hand I saw his finger on the trigger of the .30–30 that was still in the saddle scabbard" (61). She gallops off. Four shots later, after a long trek down the mountain, she starts stepping out of the Yellow Woman story, sending the horse back, and following the river to husband and children. But it will happen again: "he will come back sometime and be waiting again by the river" (62). The return to "my mother [...] telling my grandmother how to fix the Jell-O" and "my husband, Al, playing with the baby," tucks the young wife's errantry into unilinear narrative framing: "I decided to tell them that some Navajo had kidnapped me" (62). Her one regret is a matter of audience: "I was sorry that old Grandpa wasn't alive to hear my story because it was the Yellow Woman stories he liked to tell best" (62).

Through the tales retold in *Storyteller*, Yellow Woman (Kochininako) refuses any notion that the erotic disempowers her. She gains vision and power before returning to children and family. In one tale she leaves "her home / her clan" to find "the Sun House" (64) before "the winter constellations / closed around the sky forever" (66), and while fetching water at a time of hunger, is kidnapped by Buffalo Man and taken to his people. She eventually gives her life, marking the beginning of buffalo hunting and plentiful jerky for her kin (67–76). In another tale Yellow Woman leaves with Buffalo Man and, returning ten months later with twins, tries various stories of explanation (94–98). However,

> My husband
> left
> after he heard the story
> and moved back in with his mother.
> It was my fault and
> I don't blame him either.
> I could have told
> the story
> better than I did. (98)

Many Indigenous writers of the southwest embrace an ancient network of aqueous-erotic figurations from which La Llorona has emerged with her haunting/transformational double gaze. Such narratives often critique patterns of dispossession, border crisis, and ecological devastation, and point to viable paths ahead. In "My Mother Returns to Calaboz," Lipan Apache poet Margo Tamez writes of the lower Rio Grande near its Gulf mouth, and how it

> [...] smells like diesel and herbicides.
> The scene reminds me of failed gestations.
> My reproduction, the plants', and the water's,
> each struggling in the same web of survival. (322)

The narrator's mother, constantly suspected as being illegal, gets stopped by *la migra* whenever she walks or jogs on the levee. Along this levee channeling "the river's unhurried flow / to the Gulf" (323), tales of La Llorona and her drowned or poisoned children circulate, eddylike, as unspoken backstory to Tamez's recursive attentiveness to the waters of the lower Rio Grande:

> Now, I think I'd like to be running with my mother
> when she tells off *la migra*.
> Listen to the bubbling duet of water and plant life,
> listen to their sound,
> closely.
> Again and again. (323)

Again and again, what can look like gothic to border-police may sound like a bubbling of survival across deep time to others, even if it smells of herbicide and diesel in boundary waters seen as a dead zone. Something else bubbles with life.

"Voices Buried in Mississippi Mud": From Undead Ancestors to Future Children

A certain kind of "south" may be gothic, and gothic has certainly been going south. But is there an Indigenous southern gothic? This is a question taken up by Eric Gary Anderson in "Raising the Indigenous Undead." Anderson observes "that Native Southern ghost and monster stories typically eschew or downplay Euro-American gothic conventions," courting spirit-encounters in spaces known for Native removal instead. Across the Native South, "the living presence of the dead" (325) as Anderson puts it, is more beneficently empowering than haunting. Gothic was born of a moment when Europe began questioning itself (post-1764) in response to repressed knowledge and buried recognitions surrounding its expansive colonial projects. While the genre "opens up conduits for expressing otherwise inexpressible anxieties and troubles" (328), Indigenous engagements with undead ancestors call for "a counternarrative to the Gothic's counternarrative" (329). Anderson reads Joy Harjo's poem "New Orleans" as this kind of counternarrative.

Harjo (Muscogee Creek) enters a simultaneously mythic and gothicized New Orleans, listening "for evidence / of other Creeks, for remnants of voices" (43). She asserts:

> My spirit comes here to drink.
> My spirit comes here to drink.
> Blood is the undercurrent.
> There are voices buried in the Mississippi mud.
> There are ancestors and future children

buried beneath the currents stirred up by
pleasure boats going up and down.
There are stories here made of memory. (44)

Harjo's "New Orleans" listens as it speaks for undead stories and future stories
buried in Mississippi mud. But many of its voices are buried (or ominously stirred
up) by pleasure-boat waves of gothic. So the poet takes her wry time summoning
the conquistador who dominates so many Llorona tales, telling how Muscogee
peoples "knew he was one of the ones who yearned / for something his heart wasn't
big enough / to handle" (45). Consistently, the hearts of men drawn to a conquest
of Llorona cannot handle what they meet in her. It is no different here with De
Soto's quest for gold: "The Creeks knew it, and drowned him in / the Mississippi
River / so he wouldn't have to drown himself" (45). As Anderson shows, when
Harjo "raises the Indigenous undead" (332), they come with a "staying power"
and sense of repossession beyond what we know as gothic:

And I know I have seen De Soto,
having a drink on Bourbon Street,
mad and crazy
dancing with a woman as gold
as the river bottom. (46)

An unknown woman, a golden or yellow woman, a Llorona, went wherever
maize went in its crossings and symbiotic seductions of humans northward
and eastward across the Gulf and the Mississippi. Terry Ben (Mississippi
Choctaw) narrated "The Origin of Corn" (1996) in a story of how nighttime
hunters near the Choctaw Mother-mound of Nanih Waiya "heard somebody
crying [...] a lady [...] crying" for hunger (Mould 77). When they share their
game with her, she asks them to return to the mound on the next night of
a full moon, and they discover "strange seeds"—"a gift from the lady" (77).
Life-giving maize comes through a "legendary" crying woman (77), and
Choctaw storytellers steadily relate that corn arrived from across the Gulf.
Ilaishtubbee, from the Six Towns community in southwestern Mississippi,
wrote a story in Choctaw (1899) going back to "the very beginning [when]
a crow got a single grain of corn from across the great water, brought it to
this country and gave it to an orphan child" who planted it and "named
it *tanchi* (corn)" (Mould 77). Baxter York of the Pearl River Choctaw community
locates corn's origin in the migration of geese: "They pick up corn way back
in Mexico or somewhere" and "dropped the seeds" (78). Birds may give
it wings, but narratives of a legendary crying woman provide the requisite
human touch of maize's reproductive transmission.

LeAnne Howe's "The Unknown Women" draws from a Choctaw narrative published by Cushman in 1899 in which a woman appears to two hunters on a mound in moonlight, "loosely clad in a snow-white raiment," asking them to feed her (Howe, *Choctalking* 18–19). The next mid-summer, corn emerges from the mother mound. Howe's poem presents an unknown woman, *Ohoyo Chish-Ba Osh*, manifesting to two hungry Choctaw hunters "camped for the night in the swamps along the river *Ali Bamu*" (11). She appears, like Mesoamerican proto-lloronas, by the river in white, hair tassled out wildly, voicing a sound beyond representation:

> Loosely clad in the cool white mist, I wear a wreath of fragrant
> flowers in my hair and beckon for them to approach. It is then I fall
> to my knees and produce a sound I will never again utter as *Ohoyo
> Chish-Ba Osh*.
> With my own hands
> I slay all reason
> tear out my hair
> and tassel the four directions with my seed.
> The warriors inhale me. I am mercy in their mouths.
> I become Corn Woman.
> And I am mercy in their mouths. (11)

Corn Woman, "Anuk la mampa / the power of thought / represented as food" (10), always "the one you long for" (10), walks a world of her creations, "full of desire" (12).

This is where Howe's Maize-woman Host meets the settler-colonial "Taker" gassing up his Hummer on ethanol (13). She becomes transformed, made monstrous Llorona, "tortured with acids that swell my body beyond grace," studied by "Agronomists disguised as Angels," distilled to "corn whiskey" with "the nitrate plow tilling the rivers and waterways" (14). "[N]o longer beautiful," or "food for thought" (14), Corn Woman dreads the fate of the Greek deities:

> Psyche, Venus, Ego, Mercury.
> I wonder if this has already happened to me?
> Is Corn Woman a concept? Huh!
> Never real. A myth. A commodity?
> Blue Corn Chips.
> White Corn Chips?
> Red again.
> I am a buck a bag in some grocery markets. (15)

The truth of GMO maize, modified for compatibility with glysophates and other herbicides and pesticides produced by Monsanto, is the stuff of horror. But Howe's "buck a bag" Llorona speaks to the costs behind our everyday-life walking dead.

Howe draws from a Bayou Lacombe (Louisiana) Choctaw storyteller, Pisatuntema, in another narrative—about a hunter who killed a doe and awakened from a nap beside his kill to find the doe alive, inviting him to accompany her home. The hunter follows to an underworld-cave piled with deer-skins, feet, and antlers. When he falls asleep, the deer all attach hooves to his hands and feet, wrap him in hide, and place antlers on his head. The hunter awakens as a member of the cave-deer family. Howe reads Pisatuntema's story as a "lesson about creating kin with people and things who are different from ourselves" (22). It is a crossing of the gulf, and like all gulf crossings, it draws upon underworld darknesses. It is not, however, fundamentally different from the initiatory dance humans and maize did together over millennia. A maize-man marriage, like hunter with doe. The hunter does not abandon his partner here, but is adopted and transformed by his prey with whom his erotic relationship has kept the hunt vital. Howe reads Pisatuntema's story with a sense for its darker side: its relation to the eighteenth-century deerskin trade that decimated deer populations and the sacredness of the hunt. Choctaw stories responded to these crises that transformed all deer to bucks in a "buck a bag" colonial economy. This also happens to be the period of the gothic's emergence as a genre, and the tale speaks to global conditions that gave rise to gothic expression. Pisatuntema's tale, in its cave setting and boundary-crossing initiations, may counter-gothicize Gulf colonialism. As Howe sees it, "Pisatuntema's story explains that the deer are fighting back" as the doe "lures the hunter into the underground and transforms him" (22), saving their relationship and future children.

In 1909, the Bayou Lacombe Choctaw woman Heleema (Louise Celestine) told a story of the *okwa nahollo* who "dwell in deep pools in rivers and bayous" and whose skin is "light in color, resembling the skin of a trout" (115). She spoke of a spot near Abita Springs known for harboring *okwa nahollo* who would seize swimmers and "draw them down into the pool to their home, where they live and become *okwa nahollo*" (115). Those dragged away have their skin turn white and "learn to live, eat, and swim in the same way as fish" (116). People adopted by *okwa nahollo* may surface when their dear ones wail songs to them, but cannot leave the water. Perhaps something of these adoptive forces inhabits Kate Chopin's *Bayou Folk* (1894) and its canonical story, "Désirée's Baby," in which readers glimpse a bayou Llorona figure who—with her baby—may have become *okwa nahollo*.

In Chopin's tale, Désirée appears as a foundling toddler "left by a party of Texans" on the Valmondé plantation (1). The adopted border-child grows up and marries Armand Aubigny, whose plantation home serves as gothic space: the oaks "shadowed it like a pall" (2). When their baby is born darker than either parent, Armand blames his bride for the racial taint, but the text has its own things to say. Desolated, Désirée leaves the plantation: she "had not changed the thin white garment nor the slippers which she wore" (5). With "hair [...] uncovered," she takes the baby through brambles that "tore her thin gown to shreds" and "disappeared among the reeds and willows that grew thick along the banks of the deep, sluggish bayou; and she did not come back again" (5). "Desirée's Baby" leaves readers to intuit a suicidal/infanticidal disappearance. Désirée becomes Llorona in white by the waterside, betrayed and abandoned. She doesn't wail only because her text does the wailing for her from the bayou. Perhaps Désirée's baby found a home among the *okwa nahollo*, with the Choctaw of Lacombe or with Jesmyn Ward's cross-bayou ancestors, or somewhere on the Cane River of Natchitoches Parish. Chopin had likely read Alfred Mercier's *L'habitation Saint-Ybars* (1881), in which a pregnant, light-skinned enslaved woman named Titia, slips away from the plantation by joining an Indigenous group encamped nearby. They adopt her and meet "the friendly tribe of the Choctaws, who waited for them at the Bayou Lacombe" (95). After Titia gives birth and her baby girl is bundled up at the plantation doors for the mademoiselle's discovery, everything follows a predictably gothic script: a sudden hurricane, then trauma after tropical trauma accompany the girl, Blanchette, becoming woman across a hyper-materialized but never quite legible color line [...] a world of everyday gothic.

These are some of the Gulf borderwaters of La Llorona—from the Rio Blanco to the Rio Grande to Bayou Lacombe and the Mississippi—"older than the flow of human blood in human veins" as nineteen-year-old Langston Hughes wrote on his way south to Mexico (4). The Cihuateteo and Lady of Maltrata, Xtaj and Xpuch and the Maya Yellow Woman (Xq'anil), Cihuacoatl's wailing sixth omen, all speak from that flow, their voices overcoming blockage. We encounter something of La Llorona in Gloria Anzaldúa, Sandra Cisneros, and Leslie Marmon Silko, and in Joy Harjo, LeAnne Howe, and Kate Chopin. A nepantlera of double being-ness bound up with the reciprocal bioengineering of humanity and maize, La Llorona seeks her children—birthed and adopted—buried in Rio Blanco clay, Rio Grande sands, and Mississippi mud.

Chapter 2

PLANTATION ENTANGLEMENTS: GULF AFTERLIVES OF SLAVERY

One of the things I think is true, which is a way of thinking about the afterlife of slavery in regard to how we inhabit historical time, is the sense of temporal entanglement, where the past, the present, and the future are not discrete and cut off from one another, but rather that we live in the simultaneity of that entanglement. This is almost common sense for black folk. How does one narrate that?

> Saidiya Hartman, quoted in Claudia Rankine's *Just Us*

[...] look, neighbor, there is a very easy way to trap the rabbit. For this you will have to make a doll of beeswax and put it in the path where the rabbit goes.

> Anastasio García, in George Foster's *Sierra Popoluca Folklore and Beliefs*

Gothic, according to Richard Gray, is a means by which the secret history of a culture is told, the repressed revealed, the monstrous encountered, and boundaries crossed (37). The Gulf world presents an archive, both fabulous and gothic, of our secret histories and boundary-traversing traumas. Its hyper-racialized space produced a critical "double-consciousness" (3) as W. E. B. Du Bois memorably presented it, haunted by recognition that the ruling archive was partial and false since in this postplantation space of thick entanglements "[t]he price of culture is a Lie" (144). Just as the first gothic novel appeared in London in 1764, the Gulf's north shores faced accelerating pressures, spurred on by political revolution (1776), the cotton gin (1794), and the Louisiana Purchase (1803). Steady violence accompanied Jacksonian-era expansion of the plantation system over a twenty-five-year period from 1821 to 1846. Jackson's victories in the Creek War (1813–14) and the Battle of New Orleans (1815) set the stage. Then, in rapid succession, with Spain's sale of Florida (1821), the Indian Removal Act (1830), the Second Seminole War (1835–42), and the Invasion of Mexico (1846), the whole US Gulf South became a site of accelerated investment in slave-produced cotton culture. All while slavery was abolished in Mexico (1829). Indigenous peoples faced genocide and removal, slave markets expanded, and the more ethnically fluid frontier spaces between La Florida and Tejas were recharted. Anglo-Protestant notions of "the impassable gulf between the races" created by God became dogma in the US south and gripped the nation as an intensely racialized plantation belt hit expansion mode. Gothic expression proliferated with plantation space.

The new nation's gulf-ideations appear most clearly in Chief Justice Roger B. Taney's *Dred Scott* ruling (1857), answering what the Court determined to be at question: "Can a negro whose ancestors were imported into this country, and sold as slaves, become a member of the political community formed and brought into existence by the Constitution of the United States?" (17). The Court's answer was *no* since the Union sought by the founders was built on an evident but never explicitly named internal gulf: racialized chattel slavery. From determination of representation "by adding to the Whole Number of free Persons […] three-fifths of all other Persons," to guarding state jurisdiction over "importation of […] persons" through the year 1808, and assurance that "Person[s] held to Service or Labour in one state" would remain legally bound upon escape to another state, the US Constitution provided an implicitly racialized charter for the nation. The Naturalization Act of 1790 clarified things, limiting citizenship to "free White person[s] […] of good character." Discourses of racial polygenesis prevailed across the plantation belt. Louisiana University medical professor Samuel Cartwright's diagnosis in 1851 of "drapetomania, or the disease causing negroes to run away," provides infamous example. According to Dr. Cartwright, this "is as much a disease of the mind as any other species of mental alienation," with a prescribed cure: "whipping the devil out of them." Gulf medicine, law, society, and thought took increasingly binary shape around racial figurations in the early United States. From Dred Scott (1857) to *Pace v. Alabama* (upholding prohibition of interracial marriage, 1883) to *Plessy v. Ferguson* (1896), the Court affirmed a foundationally split place.

Black writers have steadily traversed entanglements of experience and perception unknown to white society. From its beginnings, African American writing has been a mode of modern gulf expression. Mindful of how "Slavery has fixed a deep gulf between you and us" (176), Reverend Henry Highland Garnet's "Address to the Slaves of the United States of America" (1843) called for insurrection. Fugitive slave narratives adopted gothic strategies, as Teresa Goddu has shown, to initiate white readers into the nation's plantation architectonics. Frederick Douglass, in his 1845 memoir, pulled readers with him to witness his Aunt Hester's shrieks under the lash:

> It was the blood-stained gate, the entrance to the hell of slavery, through which I was about to pass. It was a most terrible spectacle. I wish I could commit to paper the feelings with which I beheld it. (18)

In *My Bondage and My Freedom* (1855), Douglass recounted early separation from his mother and how, "with the impassable gulf of slavery between us during her entire illness" (156), he was unable to see her even at her death. Harriet Jacobs' *Incidents in the Life of a Slave Girl* (1861) insisted "[t]he secrets of slavery are concealed like those of the Inquisition" (367), bringing "a curse to the whites as well as to the blacks" (383). She reveals how her master's sexual predation drove her to a relationship with a young white man, though, as she writes, "I knew the impassable gulf between us" (385). Nevertheless, in her text of curses, entrapments, and secret monstrosities, Jacobs faced an initiatory need to bring readers along, even to apologize for the knowledge imparted: "Pity me, and pardon me, O virtuous reader! You never knew what it is to be a slave; to be entirely unprotected by law or custom; to have the laws reduce you to the condition of a chattel, entirely subject to the will of another" (386). Here, nineteenth-century American gothic meets today's critical race theory. Freedom gets incubated through seven years of hiding in her grandmother's attic crawl space, a "loophole of retreat" into the text's birth. But Jacobs underscores how freedom required purchase too, given the Fugitive Slave Act and the plantation's national reach: "The bill of sale is on record, and future generations will learn from it that women were articles of traffic in New York, late in the nineteenth century of the Christian religion" (512).

Legacies of slave narrative, trickster fabulism, and gothic converge in James Weldon Johnson's extraordinary novel, *The Autobiography of an Ex-Colored Man* (1912). Johnson passed this fictional work off as an anonymously written autobiography documenting the life of a racial border-crosser, his preface announcing: "the reader is given a view of the inner life of the Negro in America, is initiated into the 'freemasonry,' as it were, of the race" (vii). Johnson's narrator becomes "ex-colored man" following a lynch-scene of spectacle terror in Georgia at which he witnesses "a human being [...] burned alive" (88). The text testily acknowledges "men of liberal thought who do not approve lynching," but notes how such southern "liberals" must preface their positions in accord with "the 'great and impassable gulf' between the races 'fixed by the Creator at the foundation of the world'" (89). This gulf-ideation's longevity provides evidence enough of a national undeadness, but the novel proceeds to set the stage for twentieth-century zombie fiction when its "ex-colored" narrator leaves Georgia for New York "to make a white man's success; and that, if it can be summed up in any one word, means 'money'" (91) from New York real estate and marriage to a "dazzlingly white thing" (93). "Success" reads like zombification, with its cost: "a vanished dream, a dead ambition, a sacrificed talent" (100).

West African fables and initiation tales fostered a confluent double gaze, conveying the greatest psychic threat as a loss of open-eyed (*hippikat*) composure in the face of gulf-abysses. They often narrate a way out of no way. One particularly well-traveled Senegalese tale tasks an orphan girl (Kumba) with washing a dirtied calabash in the Atlantic (Kesteloot and Mbodj 24–31). Her stepmother does not intend for Kumba to survive the journey. But Kumba's cool navigation of an occult other world helps her receive empowering eggs from a grotesquely disfigured crone in bush initiation. She traverses what Wole Soyinka calls "the immeasurable gulf of transition" (148). When the stepmother sends her own ill-prepared daughter to the bush for her eggs, the girl ridicules all she encounters, and dies there. This tale shared ancestral voicing in and through every slave-market port. MLA President Alcée Fortier's *Louisiana Folk Tales in French Dialect and English Translation* (1895) presents it with its accompanying *nyama* or energy-of-action (Hall 50–51), as a girl (Blanche) goes to a well, meets the crone, and offers water. When Blanche must later escape her home to the bayou, she is welcomed by this witch, but must promise not to disparage anything she encounters. Blanche enters a world of terrifying dismemberment: two axes fighting, two arms, two legs, and finally two heads fighting. After the crone removes her own head to delouse herself, she gives Blanche her talking eggs, bursted one by one for their riches. Blanche's sister Rose then makes the journey, ridicules all she sees, selects the wrong eggs, and faces repercussions that send her "shrieking" through the bayou (Fortier 117–19). Amidst bushes of thorns littered with body parts, such tales of New World initiation and horror open a set of passways to encounters with otherness beyond Euro-gothic containment.

"Then there will be air, space, breath": Yoknapatawpha's Gulf Impasses

In 1935, when Ellen Glasgow disparaged Faulkner for creating a "Southern Gothic school" of literary "degeneracy" with its "stew of spoilt meat" and "colors of putrescence" (3–4), she branded "Southern Gothic" with Faulkner as iconic practitioner. This came at the moment when Faulkner was doubling down on his most gothic novel yet: *Absalom, Absalom!* (1936). But it is *Go Down, Moses* (1942) that interests us for being his deepest journey into forms of undeadness beyond what the editors of *Undead Souths* describe as the boundedness of gothic (Anderson et al. 4). Applying game theory and critical race theory to a book she had previously assessed as a "baggy monster," Thadious Davis repositioned *Go Down, Moses* "among Faulkner's greatest fictional achievements" (4). Calling it "a miscegenated text, one whose form and logic resist containment and defy boundaries," she points to "shame as a feeling pervading the text" (11). If, as Édouard Glissant observed, Yoknapatawpha "reveal[s] the radical separation (that impossible apartheid) presiding over the life of the emotions in the Plantation" (66), then *Go Down, Moses* lodges deepest shame in the space's systemic denials of love, bound up in forms of narration drawn from Caroline Barr, the Black woman who cared for Faulkner from his childhood and whose death the novel incessantly grieves (Sensibar 20–21).

How to tell such a story of shame and relation, secret histories, and gulfs of consciousness? The opening story, "Was," presents hand-me-down narrative that precedes the birth of the novel's central figure, Isaac (Ike) McCaslin, who has repudiated inheritance of the plantation. Ike's enslaved uncle Turl drives the action in escape to the neighboring Beauchamp place to see Tennie, the woman he visits "every time he could slip off, which was about twice a year" (7). Turl's enslavers, his white brothers (Buck and Buddy McCaslin), give chase, with Turl relying on a gamesmanship understood as such by his brothers to contest their proprietary claims to him (Davis 8–11). Buck and Buddy's slapstick pursuit of Turl through a Yoknapatawpha creek bottom brings Ike's parents together and becomes a divinatory fetching of futures (through a game of cards). Turl's errancy from white supremacist designs hardly reads like a gothic beginning. But there is backstory to this backstory—and an accruing legacy of inheritances—moving in energies-of-action that "Was" can't contain.

The novel's second tale, "The Fire and the Hearth," sends Turl's elderly son Lucas Beauchamp along the creek bottom at night to hide a moonshine still. Readers follow in the dark, and by a "flat-topped, almost symmetrical mound rising without reason from the floor-like flatness of the valley," Lucas stumbles into Mississippian gothic architecture—"an Indian mound"—receiving an "admonitory pat from the spirit of darkness and solitude, the old earth, perhaps the old ancestors themselves," as a clod of earth and old pottery "deposited in his palm [...] a single coin" (38). This creekside gold-discovery launches journeys across time and space [...] forty-three years into the past, when the current plantation owner's birth during a flood sent Lucas past downed timber and drowning livestock to fetch a doctor. What Lucas found, upon "emerging from that death" with doctor in tow, was "the white man's wife dead and his own wife already established in the white man's house" (45). Lucas's struggle plays out over generations as he, like his father Turl, asserts his (and his family's) most basic human rights at the risk of potential lynching. Faulkner presents Lucas as gulf avatar: "not secret so much as impenetrable" (58), ever-ready to enact a "Senegambian Montague and Capulet" (62). "The Fire and the Hearth" challenges readers to the dark matter of plantation gamesmanship: what's delineated differently, not said or named, played out opaquely through doubled consciousness.

Corpses, the dead, and death rites are pervasive throughout *Go Down, Moses* and give Yoknapatawpha much of its accrued temporal and psychic entanglement. "Pantaloon in Black," with its graveyard "marked off [...] by shards of pottery and broken bottles and old brick and other objects insignificant to sight but actually of a profound meaning and fatal to touch, which no white man could have read" (129), forces confrontations with Gulf (il)literacies in a story in which ghosts present a vexing blues presence. After his wife's death, the protagonist, Rider, becomes a grief-stricken "walker" fueled by "a whole gallon of bust-skull white mule whiskey" (149). He cuts a white sawmill foreman's throat during a perpetually rigged dice game, becoming object of a lynch mob (registered voters all) and subject of a clueless sheriff's dinnertime tale to his wife. "Pantaloon in Black" speaks to extreme phenomenological instability across Jefferson's jurisdiction as county seat, both on the local scene and for the Jeffersonian nation.

In "The Old People," twelve-year-old "Ike" McCaslin, the mosaic novel's central figure, is "consecrated" (173) in blood by his Black Chickasaw mentor, Sam Fathers, after killing his first buck in the Big Bottom. A huge ghost buck appears to them on a ridge shortly afterward and is hailed by Sam as "Grandfather" in a scene illustrative of Renée Bergland's *The National Uncanny* (2000). What "the white boy of twelve with prints of the bloody hands on his face" (156) starts piecing together over campfire talk and through the novel's subsequent narrative is a deep enmeshment in desecrations repeated across Yoknapatawpha's history and through his own family's stories and silences: including the fathering of children with enslaved women and subsequent arrangement of marriages that disinherit and bind the children across racialized gulfs. Sam Fathers' parentage marks an originating pattern, as readers learn how Sam's father Ikkemotubbe had traveled to New Orleans and returned to his Chickasaw family's plantation, renaming himself Du Homme or "Doom" (158). Doom comes back from New Orleans with "the quadroon slave woman who was to be Sam's mother" and "a gold snuff-box filled with a white powder resembling fine sugar" (157): deadly arsenic with which he usurps the chiefdom from his planter-cousin, Moketubbe. Faulkner's novel presents Doom as the one who initiates the pattern of handing a pregnant "quadroon" lover to one of his enslaved men in marriage, bypassing protocols of kinship and inheritance, deflecting the plantation's toxic legacies upon Native Yoknapatwpha/New Orleans contact zones and beyond anything Anglo-America has to claim as its own. The burial of Sam Fathers, four years after Ike McCaslin's hunting camp initiation—the "blanket-wrapped bundle" placed on "the platform of freshly cut saplings bound between four posts" (239)—marks a spectral site of Yoknapatawpha's "rememory" as Toni Morison would have us see (43).

Ghost presences emerge everywhere from Yoknapatawpha's split earth. The silence an ivorybilled woodpecker leaves in the Big Woods on the verge of extinction, forests downed by the cotton and sawmill economy feeding Jefferson's court square. While two nigh-mythic animals dominate the novel's lengthiest narrative, "The Bear," its most charged human figure, the long-drowned woman Eunice, never speaks—occupying only five pages. Eunice nevertheless takes hold of sixteen-year-old Ike McCaslin's consciousness after he reads the plantation commissary ledger, written in his father Buck's hand:

> *Eunice Bought by Father in New Orleans 1807 $650. dolars. Marrid to Thucydus 1809 Drownd in Crick Cristmas Day 1832.* (253)

What Ike pieces together from his uncle Buddy's corrective entry, "*Drownd herself*" (254), is that Eunice stepped into that icy Christmas creek after learning of her daughter Tomy's pregnancy by the McCaslin who owned and impregnated them both. Tomy died while birthing Turl six months later: "*Jun 1833 yr stars fell*" (255). Knowing that his grandfather Carothers McCaslin was Turl's father, Ike realizes Eunice was purchased in New Orleans to be his grandfather's "fancy girl" and paired with one of his grandfather's enslaved men (Thucydus) after becoming pregnant with Thomasina (Tomy). Aware that Turl was his father's enslaved half brother, Ike goes speechless on realizing Carothers McCaslin had fucked "*His own daughter. His own daughter. No No*" (257). We doubly underscore Thadious Davis's sense for how Eunice entered that creek with "an anger so profound that the only imaginable outlet was destruction" (111). And we follow Jay Watson's *William Faulkner and the Faces of Modernity* (2019) for its strong presentation of Eunice as iconic self-affirming/destructive grandmother of Yoknapatawpha (159). We must counter, however, Watson's presentation of an awakened Isaac McCaslin, who—through Eunice's act—"becomes an Ike who remembers [...] [and] belongs in her genealogy of resistance" (278).

Yes, Ike attempts reparation when he travels with cash to give to Turl's daughter in an Arkansas tenant cabin. But facing her husband in his "ministerial clothing," Ike launches into what Watson elsewhere has called a "gothicizing" white panic, as he harangues his Black in-law pushed out-of-law:

> Dont you see? This whole land, the whole South, is cursed, and all of us who derive from it, whom it ever suckled, white and black both, lie under the curse? Granted that my people brought the curse onto the land: maybe for that reason their descendants alone can—not resist it, not combat it—maybe just endure and outlast it until the curse is lifted. Then your people's turn will come because we have forfeited ours. But not now. Not yet. Dont you see? (265)

Isaac McCaslin, even when he would relinquish title to the land and offer reparations to Turl's children, uses the curse-motif to retain entitled relations to the space in a falsely virtuous way. For Ike, this is a curse to be endured until lifted passively, almost by way of what Martin Luther King called "the myth of time" (*Testament* 295). Ike's gothicizing curse on the land is doubly pernicious for how it aligns with Faulkner's 1956 *Life* Magazine essay "A Letter to the North: William Faulkner, the South's Foremost Writer Warns on Integration—Stop Now for a Moment."

In counterpoint to this breathless panic, the mosaic modalities of *Go Down, Moses* carry traces of Yoknapatawpha's composite integrations. In the novel's penultimate section, "Delta Autumn," an Indigenous tale provides back-structure to the story. The core tale, as Earnest Gouge (Muskogee Creek) narrated it in 1916 goes like this: a woman approaches a hunter with her child, revealing she is a doe whom he "killed" on an earlier hunt. If he honors their secret, wife and child will stay with him and bless him. If he spills the secret, they transform and disappear into the wilderness (86–88). It is a tale of marriage and responsibility to the other, like Pisatuntema's Choctaw "Hunter in the Deer Cave," and like widespread West African (and Acoma Pueblo) tales of hunters and Buffalo-women. The friends of Isaac McCaslin's young kinsman, Roth Edmonds, know "he's got a doe in here [...] that walks on two legs. [...] Pretty light-colored, too" (321). When she appears in camp with a newborn, seeking her lover, she finds Uncle Isaac, who goes full gothic on her upon discerning her African ancestry: "the pale lips, the skin pallid and dead-looking yet not ill, the dark and tragic and foreknowing eyes. *Maybe in a thousand or two thousand years in America, he thought. But not now! Not now!*" (343). Ike disavows kinswoman and child, and (like his grandfather) encourages marriage to a Black man: "That's the only salvation for you—for a while yet, maybe a long while yet. We will have to wait" (345). Although the lovers traveled to New Mexico after their initial encounter (341), "Delta Autumn" forecloses frontier possibilities in order to wait out old curses on space with "no elevation save those raised by forgotten aboriginal hands as refuges from the yearly water and used by their Indian successors to sepulchre their fathers' bones, and [where] all that remained of that old time were the Indian names on the little towns and usually pertaining to water—Aluschaskuna, Tillatoba, Homochitto, Yazoo" (324–25). The land's "yearly water," risen from "the Yazoo, the River of the Dead of the Choctaws" (324), marks loop-temporalities beyond calls to wait.

At the end of *Go Down, Moses* (in the story bearing the novel's title), the body of Lucas and Mollie Beauchamp's grandson, Samuel Worsham Beauchamp, comes home from Chicago by train, with "shirt and trousers matching and cut from the same fawn-colored flannel" (351). He is the unclaimed fawn sent away from the hunting camp, brought back in death from an Illinois electric chair: "Pharaoh got him," Mollie intones, "Sold him in Egypt" (353). White Mrs. Worsham reassures the anxious (Jeffersonian paternalist) lawyer Gavin Stevens in the wake of Mollie's sorrow song, "It's our grief" (363). But her claim of possession, along with the song's vibratory power, sends the white lawyer into the night, fleeing the spiritual's ancient witness: "*Soon I will be outside*, he thought. *Then there will be air, space, breath*" (362). Eunice's great-great-great-grandson's body is brought home from the Illinois penitentiary to be buried in the plantation cemetery. And it is the Yoknapatawpha lawyer who had co-sponsored the burial collection who now can't breathe, who can't orient himself in relation to faces of modernity that seem at odds with his University of Heidelberg education.

When Faulkner claimed the Nobel Prize eight years after the publication of *Go Down, Moses*, he spoke for the walking dead: "There are no longer problems of the spirit. There is only the question: When will I be blown up?" (649). Such a statement from a Mississippian in Sweden aimed to keep the energies of Eunice's icy Christmas action in endless loop, like the hearse's "circling" with the body of her great-great-great grandson around "the Confederate monument and the courthouse" (363) at the end of *GDM*: the native son, the fawn, brought home. Faulkner's message of gradualism concerning Black citizenship in the pages of *Life* in 1956—"Stop now for a moment [...] give him [the white southerner] a space in which to get his breath" (52)—echoes Ike's panic ("not now. Not yet") and Gavin Stevens' flight into the dark. Fear of being blown up here is something else: Gulf anxiety and shame, awareness of states sustained by terror. Faulkner would refuse W. E. B. Du Bois's 1956 invitation to debate on the steps of the courthouse where Emmett Till's murderers were exonerated (Moreland 80–82). Martin Luther King was already preaching to his Dexter Avenue Baptist congregation on "the white man who refuses to cross the gulf of segregation [...] [who] thinks segregation is a part of the fixed structure of the universe." King's sermon, "The Impassable Gulf" (1955), mapped Gulf terrain cosmically. So does *Go Down, Moses* with its gothicized impasses and undead mosaic.

"Back to Veracruz": States of Necrosis in *The Death of Artemio Cruz*

Faulkner's Isaac McCaslin and Gavin Stevens hit a wall in 1942. Martin Luther King challenged that wall in 1955. Revolution in Cuba (1959) and student unrest against Mexico's one-party regime (1968) added to the region's conflict. Carlos Fuentes' *La muerte de Artemio Cruz* (1962), written in Havana and Mexico City from 1960 to 1961 and hailed as a cornerstone of the Latin American

Boom, comes from this Gulf cauldron. Published in the year of Faulkner's death, *La muerte* channels a posthumous Faulknerian presence. Harold Bloom found Faulkner's undead presence in its pages so disturbing that he spoke condescendingly of Fuentes's best-known novel, assessing *The Death of Artemio Cruz* (translated in 1964) as "excessively derivative" with "an anxiety of influence that Fuentes lacks the strength to surmount" (2). What we underscore, however, are deliberately tapped postplantation anxieties that Fuentes addresses in a cross-Gulf gothic: anxieties of combined African, Indigenous, and European influence that American institutions have lacked the strength or vision to read and assess in an integral manner.

Fuentes created Artemio Cruz and his Veracruz birthplace on the Cocuya hacienda at a moment when modern Mexico thought itself distanced from African roots. Cruz's battlefield success during the Mexican Revolution allows his marriage into a wealthy *criollo* family to become landowner, newspaper magnate, and opportunistic businessman. Up to the final sequences of the novel, Artemio Cruz appears—according to Marco Polo Hernández Cuevas—"as a 'mestizo' oblivious of his African family tree," participating in an ideology of mestizaje intent on "the cleansing of blackness from the population" (180). *The Death of Artemio Cruz* defers its gothic secret—Cruz's birth "in a Negro shack" (268)—in a narrative of racial passing that returns an erased Africanity to the national imagination even as it casts a Veracruzano of African descent as its protagonist villain. Fuentes presents Cruz as symbol of revolutionary ideals betrayed, and with this figure renders Mexican monstrousness in gothic manner: simultaneously perpetuating and critiquing master narratives of Euro-criollo supremacy. Having described Faulkner as "the only baroque writer in the U.S.," Fuentes insisted on the necessity of baroque modes on a cross-cultural frontier: "When there are established truths, accepted by all, one can be classical. When there is no stable truth, we have to be baroque" (quoted in Cohn 31). This legacy imparted by Fuentes amounts to a more south-of-southern way of saying *gothic*, layered over the triracial algebra of eighteenth-century *casta* paintings and the grand baroque of the national poet, Sor Juana Inés de la Cruz (1648–95).

The Death of Artemio Cruz is among other things a racial passing novel registering how a protagonist symbolic of the underclasses enters the apex of a power structure built on an ideology of *mestizaje*. Through this vision of "*La raza cósmica*" (1925), championed by José Vasconcelos, Africans recede from the patrimony and the gene pool through their mixture with supposedly more advanced types:

> In this manner, for example, the Black could be redeemed, and step by step, by voluntary extinction, the uglier stocks will give way to the more

handsome. […] And in a few decades of aesthetic eugenics, the Black may disappear, together with the types that a free instinct of beauty may go on signaling as fundamentally recessive and undeserving, for that reason, of perpetuation. (Vasconcelos 32)

Indigenous pre-Hispanic glories may be embraced as historic matrilineage, but contemporary Indigenous lives, languages, and values (and everything African other than fondness for "La Bamba" and Veracruz cuisine) find displacement, moving toward "that new race to which the White himself will have to aspire with the object of conquering the synthesis" (32). What was mobilized with *the cosmic race*, as Jairo Eduardo Jiménez Sotero writes, was a means "of preserving only the culture and traditions of the 'advanced' civilizations," erasing or appropriating all else in "racist manner" (47–48).

It fits a Gulf logic that a *jarocho* is protagonist-scapegoat of a novel of the Mexican Revolution's betrayals. The word *jarocho* signifies someone from Veracruz, a state (and port) that trafficked in the slave trade on such a scale that Africans outnumbered Spaniards in colonial New Spain and gave the colony the second largest slave population in America by the end of the sixteenth century (Bennett 18). "Disparagement is embedded in the etymology of the term," traceable to Andalusia and to Arabic *xara* (feces), marking whoever shoveled shit from stalls: the enslaved Africans of New Spain (Siemens 157). The green-eyed *jarocho* Artemio Cruz, "[w]ith wide nostrils" (4), "olive skin" and "thick lips" (36), carries traces of African identity and keeps bumping against an "accumulated rage" (3) to hold the furnishings of power. Cruz does not fit with the gringos since he has "[n]ever […] been able to think in black and white" (27) or with Mexico's *criollo* elite who insist, "It's important to know how to make distinctions" (37). He chooses the Euro-*criollo* bastion of Puebla to court his wife and her wealthy father who has "imagined himself the final product of a peculiarly Creole civilization, a civilization of enlightened despots" (44).

Artemio Cruz's trifurcated deathbed consciousness reproduces the foundational racism. Second-person narration carries the load of self-inquisition and works as the ego's cursed inheritance (bearing the influence of both Faulkner and Octavio Paz): "You will inherit the fucked mother from above; you will bequeath her down below" (137). The novel's first-person narrative remains trapped in the hospital bed's abject present, while the third-person Cruz moves through a chronicle of history, dramatic action, and imagined legacy: heirs who "will give thanks to that lowlife Artemio Cruz because he made them respectable […] because he did not resign himself to living and dying in a Negro shack" (268). In spiralling panic, Cruz considers his legacy: "a class without class, a power without greatness, a consecrated stupidity, a dwarfed ambition, a clownish commitment, a rotten rhetoric, an institutional cowardice, a clumsy egoism" (269) and drifts in deathbed memory—his own and a nation's—"back to Veracruz where he came from" (64), down "the river in its course to the nearby sea" (270).

The tamped-down Gulf secret emerges from a Veracruz plantation via song ("El Balajú) danced on a wooden platform or *tarima* amplifying the percussive steps of *son jarocho*:

> in the neighborhood of the hacienda, the Zouaves found little bands with guitars and harps that sang *Balajú went off to war and wouldn't bring me along*, cheering up their nights, as did the Indian and mulatto women, who soon gave birth to fair-haired mestizos, mulattos with blue eyes and dark skin named Garduño and Alvarez, who in fact, should have been called Dubois and Garnier. (281)

The encamped Zouaves—soldiers of French occupation (invited into Mexico by *criollo* conservatives)—meet a fandango of hacienda workers steeped in centuries of abandonment. The experience of abandonment conveyed beneath the song's exuberant spirit carries a Gulf knowledge that "in this world there are two kinds of people, motherfuckers and assholes, and we have to decide which we're going to be" (122). The jarocho musicians who sing "Balajú" understand the extractive mechanisms of the plantation system. Here, Fuentes presents a nation stuck in plantation modality in spite of the Revolution that toppled the Porfirio Díaz regime (1876–1910).

The novel's return to origins introduces the Cocuya hacienda via Yoknapatawphan atmospherics. On a morning in 1903, we see Master Pedrito "drunk again" as roosters crow "in mourning, decadent, fallen to the status of rustic servants, their abandoned yards once the pride of this hacienda, where more than a century earlier they did battle with the fighting cocks of the region's political boss" (272). Predictably, the loyal mulatto Lunero and the "Indian Baracoa" keep the perpetually drunken heir and his mother, the grandmother Ludivinia, fed. Ludivinia, self-quarantined inside the decaying house for so long that she could double for Faulkner's Rosa Coldfield, Emily Grierson, and Caroline Compson, haunts the text (and Cruz's dying consciousness) as nigh-vampiric crone. Lunero serves as nurturing uncle to Cruz, having hidden the boy in infancy from a murderous father—Ludivinia's favored son Master Atanasio—who kills the offspring of his violations and runs the mothers off the hacienda. Lunero sings the orisha-songs his own black father brought from Cuba: "All Yeye's daughters / like husbands [...] that belong to other women [...]" (280), songs full of a blues of prohibited love, even as daughters of Yeye (Yoruba for "mother") carry lineages of knowledge and a staying power. Within this continuum from Africa via Cuba to Veracruz, on the banks of a tropical river, Lunero—all moonlight and magnolia until he is pressed into labor on a neighboring hacienda—raises his nephew Cruz to the initiatory age of thirteen, beneath Ludivinia's self-sequestered gaze.

The Death of Artemio Cruz presents Ludivinia Menchaca as originating chatelaine of Cocuya immured in a hacienda where news "of the lost lands, the son killed in ambush, or the boy born in the Negro shacks" does not reach (283). But she watches her grandchild through a window: "She had seen those green eyes and cackled with joy, knowing herself to be in another young body, she who had etched into her brain the memories of a century" (283). Cruz's dying visions reveal this cackling *bruja's* invasive survival "in another young body," and as Steven Boldy argues, repetitions of history and "gestures of those long dead, are symbolically dictated by the will of this old lady" (74). The grandmother-heiress of the hacienda endures in a way that Afro-Mexican consciousness does not. Furthermore, Fuentes's handling of Black presence as a Cuban transplantation invisibilizes deeper foundations of African roots across Mexico and particularly in Veracruz. We hear how the Cocuya estate had been "cultivated by the new black—and cheap—workers imported from the Caribbean islands" (284) during Santa Anna's time, making Africans appear as a late addition, rather than at the core of colonial New Spain. Somehow, Fuentes's best-known novel simultaneously whitewashes and returns to modern Mexico's foundational blackness while addressing an undead and reempowered monstrosity.

Yoknapatawpha also haunts *The Death of Artemio Cruz* through what stands "in the center of it all, the one-story mansion" of Cocuya, and through the prose that introduces Ludivinia's memory of Atanasio:

the green-eyed son, dressed in white on his white horse, another gift from Santa Anna, galloping over the fertile land, his whip in his hand, always ready to impose his decisive will, to satisfy his voracious appetites with the young peasant women, to defend his property, using his band of imported Negroes, against the ever more frequent incursions of the Juárez forces. (284)

Ludivinia, "ninety-three years old, born the year of the first revolt, when a riot of clubs and stones was raised by Father Hidalgo in his parish of Dolores" (286), pushes the narrative's grounding back to the first cry of Independence (1810). When her drunken son (Master Pedrito) ignores his exile from the house to bring disastrous news: "They're taking away the black [...] who gives us food," she listens, "but she did not look at the ghost who had come in to speak to her; no voice which let itself be heard inside the forbidden cave could have a body" (287). She corrects him: "Not a black; a mulatto; a mulatto, and a boy" (287), claiming the boy as "flesh of my flesh prowling out there, an extension of Ireneo and Atanasio, another Menchaca, another man like them" (290). Taking possession of her grandson's consciousness, she extends the Mexican elite's ideological hold from colonial New Spain to Cruz's rise to power inside the ruling Institutional Revolutionary Party (PRI). With the impending loss of his uncle looming, young Artemio opens both barrels of a shotgun on Master Pedrito, mistaking him for the rival boss's agent come to take Lunero away. Following that spilling of blood, the boy born on Cocuya *"in a Negro shack"* (291) leaves Veracruz with a consecrated rage as much Ludivinia's as his own. When he eventually buys and restores the old hacienda, the business baron Artemio Cruz reconfirms the design of Ludivinia's undying will to power.

The Death of Artemio Cruz returns to those first cries of Independence and to origins of repressed *negritud* in a novel that speaks of the twentieth century's first great revolution from the cross-Gulf space of revolutionary Havana. As readers float beneath "the flying buzzard linked to the pull of the deepest turn of the Veracruz River" (302), with "Cruz, thirteen years old, at the edge of life [...] friend of a forgotten mulatto" (305), we follow a Gulf-bound river, as Langston Hughes would have it, "older than the flow of human blood in human veins" (4). It pulls us with Lunero assisting his sister in labor, till her moaning and the baby's cry bring "the boots [...] approaching the shack where the woman lay on the dirt floor" (306). This is the birth and death scene of Artemio Cruz, a "Balajú" of Mexico personified. What finally kills Cruz decades after escaping the murderous father's boots—his final diagnosis—is necrosis of the intestinal wall: "my intestines don't move [...] the gases build up, don't escape, are paralyzed [...] these liquids that ought to flow don't flow any more [...] they swell me up" (299). Cruz, the nation, our entire Gulf, blows up from the inside, the viscera corrupted in "fetid stench" (307). In claiming and possessing Artemio Cruz as "flesh of my flesh," an undead Ludivinia may accomplish what Vasconcelos proposed: "conquering the synthesis of the races" (32) through "aesthetic eugenics," an eviscerating *brujería* displacing its gothic stench.

"Like an Army of Ghosts Evoked by Conjure": Yanga's Errant Tribe

Any return to modern origins takes us into the entrails of the North American plantation system: nodal ports such as Veracruz, in the years when population growth in the Americas spiked global CO_2 levels (1608–12), launching what some call the Plantationocene (Lewis and Maslin, Farrier). Reforestation of the Americas—occasioned by a century of post-contact genocide, the "Great Dying" of Indigenous peoples—had a cooling effect on the whole planet. But now, the plantation system was running full throttle and generating its own nodes of resistance. The African maroon Yanga was consolidating the victories of his palenque in the mountains of Veracruz and—in disrupting the flow of goods between the key port of Veracruz and Mexico City—was drawing resolute attention from the Spanish Crown. Already, the plantation system had generated a literature of resistance in the text Yanga dictated on March 8, 1608, laying out eleven conditions for truce. Among Yanga's demands were these: that the maroons' freedom be uncontested, that a charter on the Rio Blanco be granted for their lands and town, that he be recognized as leader, and "[t]hat no Spaniard will have a house in or stay within the town excepting during the markets [...] on Mondays and Thursdays" (in Landers 134). From its initial outraged reception in the Vice-regal court, this letter serves as a proto-gothic document of successful revolt from below. Yanga organized African resistance and sought, in victory, to protect against Spanish "aesthetic eugenics" by retaining leadership of his town and limiting Spanish presence to market days. Yanga and the town he founded mark a continuous counterpoint within plantation space.

Yanga's legacy, however, became archival secret, at least until Vicente Riva Palacio's "Los Treinta y tres negros" returned Yanga to attention in *El Libro rojo* (1870). Before engaging Riva Palacio's retrieval of Yanga to Mexico's pantheon, we must acknowledge Riva Palacio's relation to another Mexican national hero, Vicente Guerrero—the author's grandfather. *El negro* Guerrero—the Independence leader of African descent who rose through the ranks under Morelos to become the last rebel general in the field—built the Army of Three Guarantees (Independence, Catholicism, and abolition of racial distinctions) and outlawed slavery on becoming Mexico's second president. As Alice Baumgartner observes, "Guerrero bore striking similarities to Andrew Jackson, who was running for president in the United States at the same time" (63), but "[w]hile Jackson campaigned for the equality of all white men, regardless of wealth, Guerrero fought for the equality of all men, regardless of race" (64). After Guerrero was deposed by his conservative vice president in 1829, his betrayal, capture, and execution in 1831 sent a message to men of his background: *don't overreach*. In the US, a man of Vicente Riva Palacio's acknowledged ancestry would have been considered "negro" and accorded segregated social space. Riva Palacio, however, was governor of Michoacán, a general, a celebrated author and politician with enough presidential potential that he was arrested and then exiled as consular minister in Madrid by Porfirio Díaz. Riva Palacio's "Thirty-three *negros*" marks a proud reclamation of Gulf *negritud* and a gothic critique of conservative *criollismo*.

Like Isaac McCaslin with the plantation ledgers, Riva Palacio emerged from Mexico City's colonial archives to tell a buried story. In "The Thirty-three *negros*" he notes how the Spaniards turned quickly to the African slave trade for the labor they couldn't extract from a decimated Indigenous population, and how Africans resisted by marooning in the Veracruz forest. We get a date, January 30, 1609 (after the Viceroy's refusal of Yanga's conditions of peace), and an impending battle between the maroons and forces sent to quell the uprising and to reopen the crucial highway between Mexico City and the port of Veracruz. Describing Yanga as "patriarch of that errant tribe" (357), Riva Palacio affirms the virtue of errantry in the face of extractive plantation-style systems, an errantry shared—across two centuries—with heroes of Independence. After stalemate in battle left the Spanish unable to defeat the maroons, Yanga, "the spirit of the revolution" (359), finally forced the Crown's concessions to his demands.

"The Thirty-three *negros*" concludes in fully gothic mode. Having established Yanga as an Independence leader two centuries in advance of Father Hidalgo's cry of Dolores (1810), Riva Palacio moves the narrative to Mexico City, the heart of New Spain, where anxieties surrounding Yanga's uprising were calmed by public lashings of "some blacks imprisoned for various crimes" (364). By Holy Week of 1612, however, fears of uprising had grown in a city dependent on the countryside and surrounded by a largely black and Indigenous population:

> Somebody was sure that in one of the forests on the road from Mexico to Veracruz there was a camp in which blacks were counted by the thousands. Someone said that during the cold nights in February, mysterious troops hovered around the cities like an army of ghosts evoked by conjure. Some others affirmed that when all the inhabitants of Mexico slept, from the terraces of their rooftops they had seen bonfires in the surrounding mountains that could be no less than secret signals, and had heard the wild howls of the liberated blacks. (365)

Riva Palacio focuses on a now familiar hysteria-machinery: "The governing Court stoked that fear, and security measures began to be enacted that could only increase the fear" (366). Nightly curfews during Easter Week and racialized surveillance helped a new Viceroy consolidate power amidst general panic. Everything spiked following Easter Sunday: "the Royal Court [...] simply wanted a dramatic spectacle to calm the mood and threaten the blacks" (367), and in result, "Twenty-nine *negros* and four *negras* were executed on the *same day and hour* in the city's main square" (367). Riva Palacio's text from 1870 uncovers terror staged in 1612 for a public "filling the square and the streets [...] balconies and rooftops" as "spectators awaited a terrible massacre" around "thirty-three gallows from which they hung thirty-three corpses within the hour" (367). Refusing to disperse after the hangings, the crowd lingered for "a still more repugnant second act" when "thirty-three heads were fixed on poles in the city's main plaza, with all the ornate dignity and greatness of the Royal Audience" (368).

Riva Palacio reintroduced Yanga to a national pantheon, and the African's image has been conscripted as regional icon across the state of Veracruz for his early resistance to colonial oppression (Flores-Silva and Cartwright 66–71). However, a local elite inherited the perspectives and practices of ruling power. Something profoundly undead remains from that crowd in the zocalo-navel of the capital (now the fifth largest city on Earth) gathered, as Riva Palacio makes clear, around "Corpses being punished": "those trophies of civilization hung there, until the Royal Court found it no longer possible to suffer the fetidness" (368). The story concludes in a manner that resonates across four centuries: "this is how that dream conspiracy was suffocated, in the year 1612" (368). Whether in a Mexican plaza or on a Minneapolis street, a legacy of dream-suffocations has unnerving staying power.

In a world where " [t]he price of culture is a Lie" (Du Bois 144), the most effective response may be to "lie up a nation" as one of Zora Neale Hurston's Florida informants asserted (19). Gothic writing across the region has worked to ghost the (mono)cultural lie, exposing its fetid horrors and spectral afterlives. Occulted voices of Gulf counterpoint have always spoken back across plantation space and from urban docks and markets—in fabulation and music [...] via spirituals, blues, and *son jarocho*. The sugar haciendas and cattle ranches that spread through and across Veracruz from the conquest into the mid-eighteenth century were not the cotton plantations of the nineteenth-century US Gulf Coast fed by an internal slave trade routed through New Orleans. Nor were these spaces the same as the sugar and indigo-producing *habitations* of Creole Louisiana. But significant patterns of plantation relations took shape across time and space, as theorists of the greater Gulf world (from Benítez-Rojo to Glissant) have noted. In the US, slave narratives and gothicized passing novels sought to "haunt back" and to expose the lie of an impassable racial gulf. The prose and vision of Faulkner's Yoknapatawpha dove into entanglements of a composite culture in a manner that simultaneously opens up and shuts things back down: *Not yet. Not now.* Yoknapatawpha's modernist gothicism exposes the extreme instability of its region's binary structures of identity and its secret histories in a prose that goes baroque with llorona-soundings (heard or imagined): Eunice, doe-women, Molly Beauchamp's "Go Down, Moses." Across the Gulf, writing from Mexico's similarly stratified but Catholic society, Carlos Fuentes's mode of gothic followed a Yoknapatawpha model. On Cocuya, the planter class and Hispano-supremacy hold on, even across the twentieth century's first great revolution. The price of (mono)culture remains a eugenic lie, steadily and often spectacularly sacrificial, as Riva Palacio demonstrates. Whether in binary (southern) gothic manner or in more baroque (tropical) patterns, similar impasses and hauntings shape our borders, similar suffocations or deferrals of dreams. And the price in our nationalist fictions is that messages of state care and accountability also lie […] especially when they deny our shared gulfs.

Chapter 3

GULF ATMOSPHERICS: HURACÁN AND THE VISCERALESS STATE

[...] this is what you do when you can't afford an abortion, when you can't have a baby, when nobody wants what is inside you.

Jesmyn Ward, *Salvage the Bones*

Tell me, oh tell me, oh tell me
how many creatures you've sucked dry?
Not a one, not a single one,
it's only you now I want to try.

"La bruja," *son jarocho* sung by Salma Hayek in *Frida*

When Patricia Yaeger wrote in *Dirt and Desire: Reconstructing Southern Women's Writing, 1930–1990* that "the foundation or basis for this world is made out of repudiated, throwaway bodies that mire the earth" (15), she could have been addressing legacies further south and across deeper time. Peoples of the Gulf have long been reduced to the "bare life" conditions articulated by Agamben, "precarious life" per Judith Butler, "the biopolitics of disposability" as Henry Giroux observed (via Foucault) in the aftermath of Hurricane Katrina (175). Gulf inhabitants have sustained an inner life within economies of enslavement and extraction (gold, sugar, cotton, oil, tourism) and amidst an atmosphere of hyperviolence, with its heat, hurricanes, and vulnerability to climate change. Precariousness of life is revealed in contemporary gothic from the region: an embodied gnosis that Yaeger called "the unthought known" (12).

The literature of this space, for critic Richard Gray, presents a "regional rhythm" so thick with "the weather of the landscape and the weather of the mind" (26) that "'Southern Gothic' seems almost a tautology" (27). He may have been thinking of Kate Chopin's "The Storm," Zora Neale Hurston's *Their Eyes Were Watching God*, Eudora Welty's "The Winds," Linda Hogan's *Power*, and the flooded creeks of Yoknapatawpha. But this regional rhythm moves from sources beyond borders and beyond the gothic, stretching back to when "Heart of Sky, named Hurricane," shaped the creation of the world

(Tedlock, *Popol Vuh* 65). *The Book of Chilam Balam of Chumayel* also accounts for beginnings when "[t]he yearbearer winds / Spoke" (235) and prophesied a period of tragic destiny brought by aliens, "Christianizing us / And then treating us like animals. / That is the pain in the heart of God" that brought "Christianity here / To this country, / The plantation country / Of Yucatán" in "the year 1539" (Edmonson 242). We insist that this regional rhythm in Gulf writing reaches back to one of the ancient glyphic books that survived the colonial fires of auto-de-fé—the Dresden Codex, from Chichén Itzá (AD 1200–1250)—featuring an image known as "the Cosmic deluge": a female deity pouring a pot of water that falls as a plumed blue-green caiman devouring the world below (Vail and Aveni 11). Huracán has gained even more monstrous intensity over time and moves unconfined by borders.

We read the climate and gothic affect of two contemporary Gulf novels for how they (and their young characters) carry things nobody wants inside them, even as both books have won numerous awards for their handling of what they carry: Fernanda Melchor's *Temporada de huracanes* (2017) from Veracruz [translated as *Hurricane Season* (2020)], and Jesmyn Ward's *Salvage the Bones* (2011) from coastal Mississippi. Both novels present a mode of gothic in which tropic atmospherics, decadence, and storms play key roles: a carnival world of throwaway bodies, of creatureliness sucked up for the sheer pleasure or escapism or domineering power of it. Both suck up the language and vision, as well as the prestige, of Yoknapatawpha repurposed for their own designs. Both present an alternative Gulf power variously named La Bruja (the Witch), Katrina, or Medea. Melchor's *Hurricane Season* and Ward's *Salvage the Bones* feature a pregnant girl (thirteen-year-old Norma, fifteen-year-old Esch Batiste) facing storm seasons in rural Gulf Coast communities (La Matosa, Veracruz and Bois Sauvage, Mississippi). Both novels take what Ward describes as "narrative ruthlessness" to their Gulf encounters, engaging the grotesque, entrenched decadence, and what Cristina Rivera Garza describes as "the Visceraless State" [*estado sin entrañas*], a government that has abandoned "responsibility for the care of its constituents' bodies" while serving "the supremacy of profit above life" (4).

Within systems that treated them as disposable, enslaved Africans created communities of sustenance and solidarity, in ritual and religion, on plantations and in palenques. One narrative means of care, the Senegalese initiatory tale of orphan Kumba journeying through the bush to receive eggs from an initiatory crone, traveled not only to Louisiana but also— earlier—through Veracruz. Water and washing remain constant in this tale of critique and path-opening. On the upper Rio Grande the story features two Marias, with the father giving each girl a lamb. But the stepmother (read here as the Gulf state) slaughters her stepdaughter's lamb and sends the girl to the river to wash its carcass. As orphan Maria washes the viscera of her lamb (an allusion to menstruation akin to the dirtied calabash washed in Senegal), a fish steals the entrails and swims off downstream. Maria chases, arriving at a house where she soothes a crying baby and cleans the space. When the Virgin Mary returns home, the orphan is anointed with a gold star and goes home shining. The stepsister then goes to the river with her newly slaughtered lamb. A fish steals the viscera, and the girl curses the fish. She reaches the Virgin's house, spanks baby Jesus, creates a bigger mess there, and berates the Virgin Morena for being a bad mother. This Maria receives a pair of horns. The tale's allegorical turns have prophetic staying power, envisioning a postplantation state complicit with racial terror, narco-terror, unnatural disaster along our borders. It slaughters the lambs of its young and sends them to wash the entrails. Observing how acts of horror shape a world in which fear works climatically to isolate, transforming "those who are afraid [...] into the ultimate tool of the status quo" (31), Cristina Rivera Garza articulates how such tales of folk-dissensus can help "to bring back into play, and in another way, 'what can be perceived, thought and done'" (9). This viscera-washing initiation tale and the Gulf's border-traversing weather of landscape and mind guide our reading of Fernanda Melchor's *Hurricane Season* and Jesmyn Ward's *Salvage the Bones*, both of which present pregnant teens undergoing tests of passage in the face of storms and structural impasse.

"A Terrible Beauty is Born": Fernanda Melchor's *Temporada de huracanes*

Since the regional weather of Gulf landscapes and minds hardly stops at the Rio Grande or Florida Straits, how do we situate our tropical storms and loop-rhythms? Such questions have troubled critics of Mexican and US literatures, with Mexican reviewer Concepción Moreno arguing of Melchor's novel, "if we have to stamp it with a genre, we can say it is tropical gothic, much in the style of the characters of William Faulkner." Lucinda Garza Zamarripa's "De Misisipi a Veracruz: La influencia del gótico sureño en *Temporada de huracanes* de Fernanda Melchor" also observes cross-Gulf currents in Melchor drawn from "key elements in the writing of Faulkner and McCarthy, the narration's frenetic and enveloping flow of consciousness, its characters living in marginalized decadence, and grotesque situations that force readers to face social realities raised to an extreme," shaping "our own tropical gothic" (58). This heated climate carries its anxieties of influence and contagion, needs to delineate between a south and further south, our own and the other's [...] somewhere between Mississippi and Veracruz.

Sentences in *Temporada de huracanes* (2017) can swirl for pages, picking up velocity and spin, unrestrained by paragraph structure. Four different points of view frame—like the cardinal points invoked for millennia by Gulf peoples—the communal eye of this storm: the murder of *La bruja* in a true crime story fictionalized by Melchor in the pueblo of La Matosa. Gulf atmospherics drive the novel, moving Antonio Ortuño to speak of "the climate of hyperviolence and despair in which thousands of children and youth live in Mexico," and Julian Lucas to observe in his *New York Times* review that the crime here "is not an act but an entire atmosphere" through which Melchor's subject is revealed as "the inner life of misogynist violence [...] the collective mythmaking that sanctions such crimes or makes them disappear." A single scene from La Matosa's highway cantina sets the tone of thumping cumbia music and raucous laughter:

> a bottle of beer growing warm in their hand and the hum of the ceiling fan slicing through the thick heat radiating from their bodies, and the cassette player, *za-ca-ti-to pal conejo*, blaring next to the lit candle, *tiernito-verde voy a cortar*, beside the picture of San Martín Caballero, *pa llevarle al conejito*, and the aloe vera tied with a ribbon soaked in holy water, *que ya-empieza desesperar, sí señor, cómo no*, and the aguardiente to rouse the green-eyed monster, the Witch had explained, to deflect the bad energy back onto the one who deserved it, the one who'd dished it out. (14)

This is homeopathic work launched with its initial "protection": a lit candle, the saint, the aloe and aguardiente set out to deflect the text's obscene distillations of Gulf experience. But even these medicines go awry, since we are all entangled in the bad energy and get what's coming our way. *Hurricane Season*, as David Kurnick noted in the *Sydney Review of Books*, comes supersaturated in the planet's "social ills—misogyny, transphobia, homophobia, racism, neoliberal rapacity," but carries an energy different from the ethos of liberal politics.

Melchor opens in May heat with slingshot-toting boys stalking an irrigation canal, stepping into "a stench that made them want to hawk it up before it reached their guts, that made them want to stop and turn around" (3). What swirls around their discovery—the vulture-pecked corpse of the village *Bruja* floating in the canal— is the entangled decadence of La Matosa, whose inhabitants work in the sugarcane or survive on what travels the highway, selling beer, empañadas, or sex to truckers, oilmen, and narcos moving between Villa (the Port of Veracruz) and the oil fields. The murdered Witch at the center of *Hurricane Season* may be all that is left of the peoples' alternative health care, counseling, spirituality, or social protection. Clients took their "bad vibes" (14) to her, and she purged them. In a space where daily proneness to horror petrifies and isolates people, the Witch had presented a counterforce.

Readers begin to recognize that the Witch is a transgender woman who grew up in the shadows of her mother's (the Old Witch's) cures and clientele. Older women in La Matosa recall a young girl, "her frizzy, matted hair, her tattered dresses or her massive bare feet," a girl "so tall, so ungainly, as spry as any boy" (10), addressed in second person: "you, retard, or you, asshole, or you, devil child, if ever the Witch wanted her" (5). After the hurricane of 1978 and the "black sludge that swamped everything in its path" (16), the girl emerged in mourning, "in the brain-frying heat [...] that weirdo dressed in black [...] like those cross-dressers [...] at the Villa Carnival" (17). In this novel of violent sexual obsession, its most sublime eroticism comes from projections placed on that "weirdo" as young canecutters drink in the cantina and reimagine the Young Witch's gaze on them by the river earlier in the day when they were

> straddling the trunk of the fig tree suspended over the warm dusk waters, hollering and hooting, toned legs swinging in unison, shoulders all touching in a row, backs lustrous like buffed leather, shiny and dark like the seeds of a tamarind [...] skin glistening and wet and alive [...] taut and firm like the tart flesh of unripened fruit, the most irresistible kind, her favorite, the kind she begged for in silence (19).

The patrons of Sarajuana's cantina turn to "stories about La Llorona [...] who drowned all of her offspring in a vile killing spree" (20) to complete their self-portraits and regain narrative control.

Throughout La Matosa, Grandmothers indulge their sons and grandsons at the expense of daughters and granddaughters, nicknaming, for example, a granddaughter "Lagarta" for being "an ugly dark-skinned, lanky thing" (35), even as the girl (Yesenia) takes pride in having "exquisite hair" rather than "fuzzy black-girl hair" (46). Yesenia/Lagarta constantly informs her grandmother how her cousin Luismi hangs out in the park with "the rent-boy homos" (39) or "at the Witch's house, at the orgies that went on there" (40). Yesenia keeps reminding her abuela how Luismi's "slut of a mother abandoned him" (28), obsessed with a new narco lover:

> the one from the video [...] the famous video that everyone keeps sharing on their phones, a video of him doing horrific things to some girl [...] they say that's what those fuckers do to the poor girls they abduct on

their way to the border: they're put to work in the whorehouses like slaves and when they're no longer ripe for the picking, they slaughter them like lambs, exactly like in the video, they chop them up into pieces and sell their meat to the roadside food stands [...] perfect for the region's legendary tamales (42–43).

Conditions for femicide accrue in scapegoating and a steady tamping down of empathy. Luismi's stepfather Munra cautions him, "You know what these vipers are like when they want to tie you down: they take a few drops of their skanky blood and slip it in your drink or your broth" (69). Keeping numb, Munra wakes hungover, unable to take "the heat of that room or the reek of his own body" (54), while Luismi stays "as blank as a TV with no signal" (55) via opioids. Communication comes in streams of obscenities, in sexual economies or beyond language as in "the work" that Munra recalls from childhood, buried in his yard: "one of those extra-large mayonnaise jars with an immense toad floating inside" so that "whoever had the misfortune of walking over the spot where the work was buried [...] the toad would begin to eat away their vital organs and fill them with all kinds of nasty things" (75). Everything eats at these characters' viscera, threatens to slaughter them like lambs, challenges empathy, and blocks passage.

The sections of *Hurricane Season* narrated from the perspectives of Yesenia (Lagarta) and Munra provide the outer bands of the coming storm, but the final two narrative perspectives move things to the center. Pregnant, thirteen-year-old Norma, with "her rosy native cheeks and look of feigned innocence" (56) as Munra sees her, faces becoming-woman in dystopian Gulf initiation. After an abortion induced by one of the Witch's late-term concoctions, Norma wakes tied to a hospital bed, with a social worker increasing the trauma: "I'm going to tell the doctor to scrape you out with no anesthesia, that'll teach you. How do you suppose you'll pay the hospital bill, eh?" (94). Even with this state torture, "the social worker wasn't able to get any information out of Norma, not even her name or her real age or what it was she'd taken or who'd given it to her or where she'd dumped what she'd had inside her, and least of all her reasons" (92). This is the very bottom of the Visceraless State, initiating Norma at thirteen, along with the novel's readers, to its "work." Norma's intention had been to travel to the port to drown herself in the Gulf, along with "that thing growing inside her" (109). But broke, hungry, and terrified, she ended up sobbing on a park bench, and approached by Luismi, she pointed to the infamous narco and his men who were following her. Luismi's instructions—"she must never, ever point at those men [...] or go asking the police for help, because those fuckers worked for the same boss" (110)—make it clear the police and the cartels are co-conspirators in a gutted space. Luismi offers Norma refuge by taking her through the canefields to a hand-built *casita* next to his mother's "cinder block house [...] lit by a single bare light bulb." There, his continually stoned state and queer tenderness help Norma avoid confessing that "the only man she'd ever kissed was [...] her mother's husband, when she was twelve and he twenty-nine" (113).

Hurricane Season contains an embedded variant of our Gulf initiation tale, one which Norma discovers (at twelve or thirteen) in reading "The Tale of Two Hunchbacks" from an illustrated book of fairy tales. Here, a hunchback loses his way in the woods near dusk and encounters a witch's coven chanting their song "*Monday and Tuesday and Wednesday, three.*" Hidden behind a rock, the hunchback pops up exuberantly with "*Thursday and Friday and Saturday, six!*" as a response (120). The witches love this three-day addition, and remove the hunchback's hump, sending him home with a pot of gold. His jealous hunchback-neighbor then goes to the woods for the coven's gifts, hides behind a rock, hears the six-day chant, jumps up and shouts "*SUNDAY SEVEN!*" (121). What "the fool who said Sunday" receives is his "Sunday seven," an extra hump added to his front—giving a pregnant look to his belly (122). Norma suddenly understands her mother's ominous warnings and her invocations to find a hardworking "decent man like [Norma's stepfather] Pepe who won't desert you with your Sunday seven" (123). However, it is the "decent" pedophile of a stepfather, Pepe, who drags Norma into more predatory evil than anything in the witches' coven (what Ike McCaslin voiced only as *no no* in response to his grandfather's rape of his enslaved daughter Tomey). Pepe's monstrously normalized internal monologue about his stepdaughter penetrates Norma's psyche and body: "it's Norma herself who asks for it [...] ever since she was a little girl you could see she'd be a wet-pussied nympho, a regular fuck machine" (125).

Norma's pregnancy sends her running from home and lost in the canefields of La Matosa, where Luismi's mother Chabela discovers her, pregnant and living with Luismi. Posing as a mentor to Norma—telling her "there's money to be made in this game" and "all you need is a tidy ass" or "better, some other bitch's tidy ass, a piece of fresh meat with the same swagger you had when you started out" (134)—Chabela appears ready to steer Norma into "the game" run by Chabela's boyfriend, the very narco who had been stalking the girl in the plaza. Taking Norma to La Bruja to get rid of the thing inside her, Chabela makes clear her own attitude to motherhood, which follows the logic of the Visceraless State: "this children business is bullshit, bull-fucking shit [...] all kids are a burden, spongers, parasites who suck the life and all your blood from you" (136). Norma's hemorrhaging after drinking the Witch's purge leads to her hospitalization and Luismi's murderous rage against the Witch. And what was inside Norma ends up in a little hole outside Luismi's shack, dug up and eaten by a feral dog.

The fourth of the narrative directions of Melchor's storm-winds takes shape from a character wholly enveloped in phallocentric toxicity: Brando only wanted "the hell out of that stinking, fag-infested town," but finds himself in jail after the Witch's murder and subject to police torture intended only to uncover the location of La Bruja's supposed riches. Bullied by his gang of park-rats since the age of twelve for never having "squirted his load inside anyone," Brando feels burdened with proving himself a man (152), and *Hurricane Season* charts his rites of passage from the "bikini-clad sluts in his mom's magazines" (154) to bestiality porn that leads him to wandering the streets at night [...] wherever stray dogs are congregating around a female in heat, finding something as he watches the dogs that can move him to "the numb languor of that divine emptiness, the calm that washed over him whenever he was able to finally purge himself of the venom filling his balls" (156).

Veracruz's famous carnival becomes the time-space where Brando finds himself amidst "the spectacle of those out-and-out queens, the vast legion of fairies and trannies who'd come from every corner of the republic" (160). This is Mexico's New Orleans, and the Witch reproduces this carnival ethos throughout the year, hosting clandestine fiestas in her basement in La Matosa with ample alcohol, drugs, and a karaoke drag show. When Brando follows his friends to the house of "that grotesque specter" (166) to snort coke or eat mushrooms, he sees things that dilate "their eyes like Japanese anime characters": the Witch shedding her black veils for "shiny colorful wigs and all sorts of costumes" (167), singing pop songs with lights and music pulsing behind her. To his shock, he sees his friend Luismi take the stage, and listens in amazement to "that skinny rat-face runt, up to his tits in pills," with "a voice so beautiful, so intense, so amazingly pure but at the same time manly" (169). Brando is wholly stunned by how Luismi's singing moves him, by Luismi's kissing the Witch in front of the farmers and young hustlers there. A sudden simultaneous obsession and hatred for Luismi leads to stupefied sleepover sex, and once Luismi shelters Norma, Brando's obsessions with "that nasty queer shit" (183) grow to murderous rage. He dreams of killing his mother, robbing the Witch, and using the money to escape to Cancun with Luismi, though Brando would eventually have to "waste that fucker in his sleep" (188). The Witch's murder comes at Brando's instigation, with Luismi suddenly eager after Norma's disastrous late-term abortion. Having found no treasure in the dead Witch's house, Brando is apprehended days later while stalking a boy at a gaming arcade, and tortured by the police for information.

When the police bust into the boarded-up second story bedroom of the Witch's house, looking for rumored treasure, the ensuing gossip comes straight out of Faulkner's "A Rose for Emily": how they found "the black mummy of the Old Witch [the Witch's mother] lying supine in the middle of the solid oak bed" (203). Other voices insist the police did find gold, and were, in turn, murdered by a rival cartel. A "they say" litany envelops the aftermath: "They say the heat's driven the locals crazy [...] and that hurricane season's coming hard, that it must be bad vibes, jinxes, causing all that bleakness: decapitated bodies, maimed bodies, rolled-up, bagged-up bodies dumped on the roadside or in hastily dug graves on the outskirts of town" (204). The horror is that these events and attitudes hardly read like fiction in a stylistically innovative work enabling, as the most potent gothic work does, "the enunciation of what 'we cannot speak'" (Eljaiek-Rodríguez 10). The original Spanish-language publication ends with the following note of acknowledgement: "To the journalists Yolanda Ordaz and Gabriel Huge—assassinated in Veracruz during the rule of the infamous Javier Duarte de Ochoa—, whose police notes and photographs inspired many of the stories that populate this *Temporada de huracanes*" (223). Governor Duarte de Ochoa resigned and fled Mexico in 2016, having gutted state pension funds for personal gain. Melchor's novel serves as a barometer: the elections of 2018 on the horizon, with the advent of Andrés Manuel López Obrador's "fourth transformation" (4T) sweeping a divided nation, and with Trump divisively installed on the other side.

Melchor concludes *Hurricane Season* with a gravedigger scene, an abuelo with his shovel waiting for the vehicle from the morgue to deliver "the faceless, sexless remnants of people [...] [and] post-op scraps from the Oil Company clinic" (207). Here, at the end, the grandfather speaks tenderly with people's remains as he buries them, "and this seemed to console them a little, to stop them going off and hassling the living" (209). He welcomes the coming rain as the first "plump raindrop landed on the hand gripping his shovel" (209). And with a sudden lightning strike, ancient Mesoamerican texts of cataclysm and renewal accord with the Grandfather's words at the brink of the mass grave:

> The rain can't hurt you now, and the darkness doesn't last forever. See there? See that light shining in the distance? The little light that looks like a star? That's where you're headed, he told them, that's the way out of this hole. (210)

In all of its violence and obscene reduction of people to consumable *carne* (meat/flesh), *Hurricane Season* presents a dark carnival of all that Gulf nations ignore. What is inside of people and systems here suffers from necrosis, as with Artemio Cruz and the fetid atmospherics of Yoknapatawpha. The old project of aesthetic eugenics does its insidious work in this canefield pueblo: Luismi, "so ugly, with […] his black man's nose and that coarse, frizzy hair, which, by the looks of things, was the norm in La Matosa" (107). Luismi's mother (Chabela), whose phone ringtone is her narco-novio's signature song—*me haré pasar, por un hombre normal*—holds herself high because she is not dark-skinned like "Big-assed black Leticia" (163) and not like Doña Tina: "the old half-breed" whose daughters "turned out even blacker and looser than her" (132). In the center of Villa the priest prays for a cleansing of "the black magic rituals and superstitious beliefs which, to the town's shame, abounded […] because of the African roots of those who lived there" (150). Readers face overheated climatic conditions of Gulf violence (especially narco and oil violence as successors of "normal" plantation violence) in a *jarocho* community. It is from a sense of apocalyptic temporality—and a desire to midwife something revolutionary carried to term—that *Hurricane Season* concludes with the first rains and darkening energies of its epigraph from W. B. Yeats' "Easter, 1916": "Transformed utterly: / A terrible beauty is born."

"An Endless Eye": Hurricane Katrina and Jesmyn Ward's Bare-Bulb Gothic

Jesmyn Ward's Bois Sauvage, Mississippi and Fernanda Melchor's La Matosa, Veracruz share more than the Gulf heat and proneness to hurricanes. The action in Ward's *Salvage the Bones* (2011) and Melchor's *Hurricane Season* swirls around people living on the margins in "bare-bulb" places (Ward 1). For critic Christopher Lloyd, "[t]he biopolitcization of southern life" in Ward's novel "evinces a kind of creatureliness that is literalized in the connections between humans and animals" (262). Though such connections have long sustained rural peoples, they may also push people onto the creaturely side of a gulf between their own conditions and assumed norms of citizenry, all exposed— as racialized—in the aftermath of Hurricane Katrina by the lack of response, and by media reports circulating white hysteria. The Visceraless State, a state of undead rapacity, seems like apt description for what Erica Edwards calls this novel's "evisceration of the distinction between human and nonhuman life […] in parallel relationship to the biopolitical operations of the state" (157).

Ward's novel opens with the narrative voice of the only girl/woman of the family, Esch Batiste, fifteen, soon to discover she is pregnant, watching her brother's pit bull China give birth, much the way "Mama had all of us in her bed, under her own bare burning bulb" (2). Like the girls sent to wash their calabashes or slaughtered lambs in Gulf initiations, Esch is an orphan: Mama died giving birth to Junior, and Daddy's care is well intentioned but insufficient. From the start, with radio reports on a tropical storm entering the Caribbean, Ward builds gothic atmosphere. She turns to a canonical model, Faulkner's *As I Lay Dying* (1930), in Esch's pride over scoring an *A* for her response to her English teacher's question: *"Why does the young boy think his mother is a fish?"* (7). Clearly Esch has been pondering similarities between Faulkner's orphaned characters and the predicaments faced by her own family in Bois Sauvage, and Ward draws on *As I Lay Dying* in an assertive way—its characters, structure, even its "cyclone"—helping "to confer on the characters in *Salvage the Bones*, through their association with Faulkner's, a dignity denied them in the post-Katrina moment" (Moynihan 551). Dignity denied, a "biopolitics of disposability" put on display in unresponsiveness to Black lives, was one revelation wrought by Hurricane Katrina (Giroux 175). More embedded in the novel than anything from Faulkner, however, is the story of Jason and Medea that stirs Esch's imagination after an assignment from Edith Hamilton's *Mythology*. Like Medea, Esch obsesses over a self-obsessed lover. Medea also becomes Katrina's storm-double, the mythic Mother who kills her children, a classic Llorona.

No climatic Gulf force works quite like Carnival season to highlight how legacies of Indigenous, European, and African peoples shape Bois Sauvage as much as they shape La Matosa. Carnival is the time when Gulf peoples assert their vision and presence most viscerally. Esch describes one of the pit bull China's newborn puppies as mewling like "the loudest Mardi Gras dancing Indian," born "chanting and singing like the New Orleans Indians, like the Indians that gave me my hair" (12). When Esch, her brother Skeetah, and Big Henry go to the grocery ahead of the storm, "[t]he heat beats at the car like Mardi-Gras parade goers" (28). The heat accrues carnival-style in heavy parade atmospherics. Mardi Gras carries what is inside the lives of Bois Sauvage: something of African, Choctaw, and French Creole forebears that white supremacy has not fully gutted, removed, or pathologized— enduring *nyama* or energy-of-action.

Other structural elements emerge, including the novel's initiatory frame. Esch's mother taught her to find the hens' "hidden eggs" (20), and the hens' efforts to hatch eggs in well-placed nests provides the backdrop for Esch's discovery of her own pregnancy. She remarks that sex is "[t]he only thing that's been easy for me to do" (22), and since the age of twelve, with whatever boy, "[i]t was easier to keep quiet and take it than to give him an answer" (23), easier to "let the boys have it"—that fruitlike "pulpy ripe heart" of "the other me" (16). When Esch and her brother encounter a car wreck on the way home from buying groceries, we come to a moment like the opening discovery in *Hurricane Season*: "a body in a ditch" (32), a "woman with [...] hair the color of a golden condom wrapper" (33). This is the tone and color palette of Esch's observed world. And as Hurricane Katrina nears Bois Sauvage, the pit bull China becomes a Medea figure for Esch, a fierce "bitch" and "a weary goddess" feeding her pups (40). When the first pup sickens from parvo-virus, Esch sees the care with which Skeetah cleans the space—"It's all contaminated. [...] Everything [...] The parvo. It's in the dirt in the shed" (59). A slow brooding intensity gathers—across the Gulf—to wash things clean.

Salvage the Bones triangulates feminine power around China, Esch, and Katrina, all given figuration via the witch-goddess Medea. After China gives birth, Manny (Esch's lover) disparages the dog's fighting future: "Take a lot out of an animal to nurse and nurture like that." Skeetah responds: "That's when they come into they strength. They got something to protect" (96). For all of the violence in *Hurricane Season*, "the black heart of Bois Sauvage" (97) harbors more collective fight, primarily because it is written from within by an author who identifies with a place where "[t]he bare bulb burns outward, shining on the dirt" (103). It is here that Esch ponders abortions more dangerous than the Witch's concoction—contemplating drinking bleach, overdosing on birth control pills, and violent blows to the stomach: "this is what you do when you can't afford an abortion, when you can't have a baby, when nobody wants what is inside you" (102). Meanwhile, Skeetah steals Ivermectin from a white farmer's barn to treat his dogs' parvovirus, and Katrina's Medea energies push shoreward, gathering howling Llorona-force, leaving Esch to ask, *"Is this what motherhood is?"* (130).

Gothic space often takes on agency, but Gulf-space tends toward extra shapeshiftings [...] via animal avatars (naguals, familiars), creaturely knowledge, and monstrosity. Here "houses [look] like possums in the dark, half caught and then left behind by the headlights" (131). Esch's father's bloody gauze-wrapped hand "looked like a webworm moth nest wound tight in a pecan tree" (132). "Junior's back is a young turtle's shell" (197). "The rapper sounds like a squirrel" (183), and "Daddy's eyes shine in the dark like an armadillo's" (212) as everything becomes something other. "'Play with the antenna,' Daddy says" (134) and the TV emits an emergent brood of sound and strange first-name intimacies—weatherman Mike's voice coming through, Katrina coming, and "Mama smiles serenely from the photo," unaware "that three years later, she will be bleeding to death in the bed" (135). Space and time spin grotesquely free. Amidst all of this pre-storm swirling, Esch attends her brother Randall's basketball game, and Manny forces his way into her bathroom stall to have sex with her on the toilet seat. Esch makes Manny engage her beyond penetration, makes him feel and know "the swell that is more than swell [...] the budding baby" (146) that turns him away "from what I carry" (147). Afterward, the toilet-flush has Esch "watch[ing] the water spin in a spiral, a baby storm" (146). The pit bull mother, China, keeps emerging as an avatar of the Medea narrative behind Katrina "coming straight for us" (155): a ferociousness with the teeth to "*make insides outsides*" and the force to "*make them know, make them know, make them know*" (171) as she triumphs in a fight with the male dog that sired her pups. China's ferocity, like Katrina's and Medea's, summons something inside Esch that refuses to be minimized. When Manny finally shows up after the scene in the bathroom stall, and denies being the baby's father, Esch "flies into him with Medea's rage" and "flew [...] into the wind on dragons" (205). Knowing her own strength, Esch can open to what's coming: "*everything will be washed clean*" (205). Katrina's washing-clean certainly makes folk know. In her aftermath, "the yacht club, and all of the old white-columned houses that faced the beach, that made us feel small and dirty and poorer than ever [...] are gone [...] completely gone" (253).

Esch understands what it means to claim a badass animal of one's own, and Ward's gothic narrative twists between creaturely fable, mythologized horror, and Gulf initiation. Although China carries something of Medea's ability to "turn the inside outside" and spill the other's guts, nothing can match Katrina. Katrina is the monster in the face of which the nation and the states of Mississippi and Louisiana visibly abandoned vulnerable citizens, providing only the evacuation robo-call eschewing responsibility: "*If you choose to stay in your home and have not evacuated by this time, we are not responsible. You have been warned*" (217). The novel turns fully apocalyptic as Katrina arrives "like a snake big enough to swallow the world" (219), "its tail wider and wider, like it has eaten something greater than itself" (236–37), moving towards Esch with its "fanged pink open mouth [...] swallowing me" (234). We hear "the hungry maw of the storm," how it "screams, *I have been waiting for you*" (230). And this monster's savagery makes Ward's characters know their own tenacity and love for each other. They make the choices Medea did not make. Every character sacrifices something dear in support of another (Skeetah loses China to help Esch) as they nearly drown in their attic and move from one rooftop to another. In spite of "the narrative ruthlessness" that Ward felt necessary in her plot treatment of the Batistes, she treats each family member with sisterly affection and respect, affirming her male characters' loyal tenacity under pressure. She manages this in a novel depicting a range of violence experienced by girls and women under the conditions of patriarchy, all while Katrina makes us know, mercilessly. However, Esch and Ward also make readers know something of the grace and power of dear ones around them.

As in post-classic and colonial-era Maya texts, Huracán carries time/space-altering force: "suddenly there is a great split between now and then, and I wonder where the world where that day happened has gone, because we are not in it" (251). Katrina's "uncompromising strength" that "made things happen that had never happened before" (248) may scour Bois Sauvage clean in certain ways, but it is a scouring "washed over with mud" (249) and "vomited [...] out in pieces" (252). *Salvage the Bones* presents its furious goddess-triad of initiation: "Katrina, the mother that swept into the Gulf and slaughtered," whose "chariot was a storm so great and black the Greeks would say it was harnessed to dragons," who "left us a dark Gulf and salt-burned land" and "left us to salvage" (255); and China who "*make[s] insides outsides*," who "*make[s] them know*" (171); aligned with Medea typologies. They merge as the disfigured egg-bestowing crone of Afro-Atlantic initiation tales, whirlwind Oya of Gulf waters and cemeteries, Huracán of Mesoamerican creation: "Katrina is the mother we will remember until the next mother with large, merciless hands, committed to blood, comes" (255). For all its harrowing experience, this remains feel-good gothic of survival in the end—while Ward's subsequent work would grow even darker, more tender and *nyama*-charged in the memoir *Men We Reaped* (2013), the novel *Sing, Unburied, Sing* (2017), and an ongoing historical novel set in New Orleans.

Even while facing considerations of self-harm and the perils of the storm, *Salvage the Bones* never makes room for the possibility of aborting "what's inside" Esch Batiste. Gulf Catholicism, patriarchy, and lack of resources are clearly part of the reason "choice" to abort does not emerge. But the initiatory narrative engages a larger choice: that Esch's own Black life, her family's life, and the Black life inside her matter. A choice asserted in a Gulf South where the right to choose no longer exists. In Katrina's aftermath, Esch's humbled father raises the belated need for prenatal care, and her friend Big Henry asserts "This baby got plenty daddies," counting himself among the men in the family (255). The text's final words, spoken to China, to the stars, to the dead mother, to Medea and Katrina and beyond—"She will know that I am a mother" (258)—claim possession of a freshly experienced power on shores very different from the mainstream Llorona tale, and with a hard-won stance amidst the split places, impasses, and raging waters of the Gulf.

Phantom Children, Specter Friends

Salvage the Bones and *Hurricane Season* convey a visceral gulf-knowledge from Mississippi and Veracruz. How do we read this knowledge in the aftermath of Coronavirus lock-downs and deaths, racial reckonings and backlash, ongoing climate catastrophe, accelerating border-violence and incarcerations? Jesmyn Ward described to *The Guardian* the moment she dropped the phone on getting a nurse's call that she was carrying a son in coastal Mississippi:

> I looked at the phone on the floor and thought of the little boy swimming inside me and of the young men I know from my small community

in DeLisle, Mississippi, who have died young. There are so many. Many
are from my extended family. They drown or are shot or run over by
cars. Too many, one after another. A cousin here, a great-grandfather
there. Some died before they were even old enough legally to buy alcohol.
Some died before they could even vote. The pain of their absence walks
with their loved ones beneath the humid Mississippi sky, the bowing
pines, the reaching oak. We walk hand in hand in the American South:
phantom children, ghostly siblings, spectre friends.

As the title of Ward's *Guardian* interview asserts, Mississippi's gulfs are the
nation's, only with a more packed and intense duration: "Raising a black son
in the U.S.: 'He had never taken a breath, and I was already mourning him.'"
   Gulf atmospherics that had never been confined to the US south shaped
the presidency of the forty-fifth president of the United States. From
the insurrection of January 6, 2021, to these early words from his candidacy
announcement speech promoting a southern border wall, Trump worked to
widen Gulf space:

When Mexico sends its people, they're not sending their best. They're
not sending you. […] They're sending people that have lots of problems,
and they're bringing those problems with us. They're bringing drugs.
They're bringing crime. They're rapists. And some, I assume, are good
people.

If gothic enunciates "that which we cannot speak" (Eljaiek-Rodríguez 13), we
may see that the forty-fifth US president was appealing to his base support
in similar manner, proudly resurfacing gulfs upon which the nation was
founded. Simultaneously, and further south, Fernanda Melchor was targeting
border walls of wealth and power within Mexico. In her depictions of despair
and hyperviolence, impunity and social dysfunction, she risked illustrating
the fears and projections of the MAGA movement, as her characters indeed
"have lots of problems." Melchor's concerns, however, remain primarily with
immediate gulfs within and beyond. She explained in a *Granta* interview
that "all my novels until now have explored what it is like to be really young
and really angry in a family that has broken up, in a country that cannot offer
you a future, in a world that's sinking." Narrating the possibility of a future
in this world may be her beyond-gothic mission, as it seems to be with Jesmyn
Ward. We are reminded again of Martin Luther King Jr's 1955 sermon on
"The Impassable Gulf" in Montgomery, how "the sin of [the rich man] Dives
was that he felt the gulf which existed between him and Lazarus [hungry
at the gate] was a proper condition of life" and "part of the fixed structure

of the universe." Reverend King ended his sermon in urgent recognition that our gulf "is now passable. But it can become impassable."

Although both are bare-bulb places, Bois Sauvage is not La Matosa, in part because it is written in first person narration by a young woman from within the internal Black experience of DeLisle, Mississippi. Despite Ward's self-perceived need to write with "narrative ruthlessness," she carries a fiercely protective love of the Batistes and of Bois Sauvage, narrating with affect, partisanship, and invested care [...] in a space where the message that "Black Lives Matter" would soon be considered far-left radicalism. Melchor's *Temporada de huracanes*, necessarily fierce and contrapuntal, moves from a gaze that accesses La Matosa from cantina gossip and from perspectives of witnesses trying to free themselves from the language of police reports, which she handles powerfully as an ex-journalist in Veracruz. The worlds of La Matosa and Bois Sauvage speak to each other across a widening Gulf where the horror of impasse and climatic catastrophe looms. We may get a shared taste of Gulf rage in the storm-summoning last curse of the famous New Orleans *bruja* Marie Laveau—as re-channeled by Zora Neale Hurston—targeting all who disrespect her dear ones: "I pray that their children who may come shall be weak of mind and paralyzed of limb and that they themselves shall curse them in their turn for ever turning the breath of life into their bodies" (197). Whether read partially as southern or tropical gothic, or as something beyond—the Gulf text's curse enunciates in lightning and thunder an unspeakably pressurized environment.

Chapter 4

CODA: "PHANTASMAL SPACE"

Monument 32, Tamtoc site, by a natural spring reservoir near the border *of San Luis Potosí and Veracruz (drawing by Maya Cartwright).*

The Gulf of Mexico has nurtured diverse life forms in the region's estuaries and deltas, bayous and rivers. Gulf peoples have been at the forefront of cultural innovations while also enduring every plague known to humankind: extreme social stratification and environmental catastrophe, conquest and pandemics, the dehumanizing effects of plantation slavery, religious and capital predation, revolutions gone awry, gutted social systems and divisiveness. We have addressed a gothic realm and something older than gothic stirred up in horror or holy-dread where psychic gulfs meet the traumas of Gulf environments and history. Our notion of gothic gulfs encompasses a region across borders and beyond spatiotemporal disciplinary divisions—where submerged histories find enunciation on glyphed stone, in dance and song, novel and tale, on movie screen or YouTube posting for whoever seeks or evades a meeting point, actual or phantasmal as it may be. Our gulfs find us. And the undead realm where "rememory" engulfs us often takes gothic form.

"What's in the past is in the past," the daughter of a genocidal ex-general tells herself at night in bed, in the family mansion as something spectral takes hold in Guatemalan filmmaker Jayro Bustamante's *La Llorona* (2019). But folk familiar with Faulkner, Fuentes, or La Llorona know better. Something from an Indigenous Split Place older than Spanish conquest seeks justice in this twenty-first century horror film. La Llorona's legend continues inspiring film directors, novelists, poets, and playwrights because it addresses ongoing traumas and anxieties experienced by children-of-the-corn. The weeping woman in Mesoamerican culture has acquired respect and instilled fear at the same time. Awareness of her haunting presence appears stronger than respect for her daughters or their land.

In Bustamante's *La Llorona*, an aging, ailing General Monteverde is freed on charges of genocide from the country's 36-year civil war, and a young Maya woman (Alma) dressed in white moves through the crowd of protesters gathered outside his mansion, as she starts work as a maid in the household after the staff has quit. Viewers gradually see that Alma (Soul) and her children were killed by the General's men and that she has emerged from death's waters for a reckoning. Alma brings a frog into the house, and the film floods with aqueous energy: a bathroom overflows, a faucet continually runs, the backyard swimming pool fills with frogs. Each scene presents a threat of drowning against a soundtrack of protesters, prayer chants, drumming, crying, and belabored breath. The insomniac general hunts the source of the crying through labyrinthine halls, firing his pistol in a panic. Finally General Monteverde's wife is possessed by Alma's perspective, witnessing her husband's murder of Alma and children in haunting cinematics. As a filmmaker working with the Llorona legend, Bustamante explains how he used Hollywood-style packaging to expose a grief so raw it remains almost taboo to exhume it: "we used the horror genre to talk about genocide, from the perspective of the genocidal dictator and interpret his house as the house of the devil" (quoted in Aguilar). It is a house of the devil that has received much outside support.

If "the gothic teaches the reader what to fear" (14), as Sarah Gilbreath Ford writes, the texts addressed in *Gulf Gothic* have done their part in making us know. These texts present fear of monstrous presences crossing boundaries in our daily lives, but their double gaze exposes another kind of panicky recognition as the effects of genocide, enslavement, and segregation are surfaced, and we see a build-up of energies-of-action (*nyama*) from a cultivated inhumanity. Something highly performative—with life-or-death stakes— moves in rememory of our spatio-temporal gulfs. In *A Ballad of Remembrance* (1962) Robert Hayden's "Veracruz" takes readers along the port's breakwater, contemplating a suicidal leap into waters that swirl out of Olmec deep time and Huracán's aqueous creation:

Here only the sea is real—
the barbarous multifoliate sea
with its rustling of leaves,
fire, garments, wind;
its clashing of phantasmal jewels,
its lunar thunder,
animal and human sighing. (19)

We enter the trans-Gulf space that summoned Edna Pontellier into the Louisiana waters of Kate Chopin's *The Awakening* (1899), breakers from which humanimal-voicings call for suicidal plunge: "*Leap now/and cease from error./Escape. Or shoreward turn*" (20). Hayden's "Veracruz" emerges as shoreward turn from "long warfare with self, with God" while remaining a gothicized colonial-era port where "marimba'd night / and multifoliate sea become / phantasmal / space" (20). His "phantasmal space" moves in submarine circuits across the Gulf in "A Ballad of Remembrance," the book's title poem in which New Orleans becomes Veracruz's spectral twin: "down-South arcane city with death / in its jaws like gold teeth and archaic cusswords" (28). Old warfare with self finds carnival street spectacle here: "Love, chimed the saints and the angels and the mermaids. / Hate, shrieked the gun-metal priestess," and history's "Contrived ghosts" taunt and conjure like abyssal shapeshifters:

As well have a talon as a finger, a muzzle as a mouth,
as well have a hollow as a heart. And she pinwheeled
away in coruscations of laughter, scattering
those others before her like foil stars. (27)

Above all, Gulf gothic is performative and unbound by Euro-gothic convention.

Evocations of phantasmal space across the region may summon millennial presences. But if traditional gothic dates to 1764 with *The Castle of Otranto*, we could claim a performative origin for modern Gulf gothic in the port of Veracruz when the Holy Inquisition banned performance of the *son jarocho* song "El chuchumbé" in 1766. Here we have the castle (the fortress of San Juan de Ulúa), the monstrosity and fear of contagion (a time and place of intense African maroon resistance), and an uncontainable erotic charge. Complaints from Veracruz noted scandalous dance-verses that mocked predatory priests for their cloaked arousal and phallic "levitation." One informant described the "Chuchumbé" to the Inquisitor as a "shaking that is contrary to all with honesty, a bad example of what you see when you mix touching, stretching arm to arm and then stomach to stomach [...] danced in ordinary houses of mulattos and people of broken race, not of serious people" (in Díaz-Saunders and Hernández 194). This insurrectionist twerking from those who wouldn't stay in proper formation testified to the peoples' truth-telling under the nose of surveillance and to how truth becomes zombie outbreak in the eyes of gutted authority. Being banned and thus obsessively transcribed, *son jarocho* songs were preserved in the Inquisition's archives. In the state capital of Xalapa on the day after Christmas of 1771, the Holy Office received a complaint about an organist in the convent of San Francisco who played the "Chuchumbé" in a medley of indecent songs (Sánchez Fernandez 41-42). Did the convent organist really play "El Chuchumbé," "La Bamba," and "El Balajú"? Or were Veracruzanos so filled with racial *xara* and/or *son jarocho* erotics that this is all they could hear from an organ that Christmas in Xalapa? Either way, it is classic Gulf gothic.

In her 2016 Super Bowl performance and "Formation" video, Houston-born Beyoncé Knowles brought the Chuchumbé's "contrary shaking" to the nation: a Louisiana and Texas-Bama *nyama* (swag) to face wider storms, with Tabasco or even El Yucateco sauces packed in a Gucci bag. Speaking for the dead of a "'Formation' Nation" with styles and choreography summoning Black Panthers and the Black Power salute of John Carlos and Tommie Smith at the 1968 Mexico City Olympics, as Riché Richardson has pointed out (100), Beyoncé also brought powerful erotic energy into play. Her "Formation" video delved even deeper into tropically gothicized vibes, simultaneously funereal and erotic, celebratory and confrontational, tapping into New Orleans music and spirit tied to the greater Gulf, while opening and closing with reimmersion in the energies/traumas of Hurricane Katrina. The closing images of "Formation" leave viewers in Gulf waters between initiation and drowning: Beyoncé lying in four-directional cruciform stillness atop a sinking New Orleans police car, floodwaters bubbling around her as she becomes Gulf *Sirena*. "She establishes contact between the dead and the living," Valérie Loichot observes, becoming liminal siren-figure, positioned "in the ambivalent place between threat and salvation, since she has the power to deliver both: she can drag people underwater and bring them back alive to the surface" (133). This "'Formation' Nation" moves in phantasmal space beyond easy nationalisms or historicized temporalities, ruled by La Sirena, La Llorona, Xtaj and Xpuch, and inhabited by undead voicings from gulfs between us.

WORKS CITED

Agamben, Giorgio. *Homo Sacer: Sovereign Power and Bare Life*. Translated by Daniel Heller-Roazer. Palo Alto: Stanford University Press, 1998.

Ajuria Ibarra, Enrique. "Ghosting the Nation: La Llorona, Popular Culture, and the Spectral Anxiety of Mexican Identity." *The Gothic and the Everyday: Living Gothic*, edited by Lorna Piatti-Farnell and Maria Beville, 131–51. London: Palgrave Macmillan, 2014.

Anderson, Eric Gary. "Raising the Indigenous Undead." *The Palgrave Handbook of the Southern Gothic*, edited by Street and Crow, 323–35. London: Palgrave Macmillan, 2016.

Anderson, Eric Gary, Taylor Hagood, and Daniel Cross Turner, eds. "Introduction." *Undead Souths: The Gothic and Beyond in Southern Literature and Culture*, edited by Anderson, Hagood, and Turner, 1–9. Baton Rouge: Louisiana State University Press, 2015.

Anzaldúa, Gloria. *Borderlands / La Frontera: The New Mestiza*. San Francisco: Spinsters/Aunt Lute, 1987.

———. *The Gloria Anzaldúa Reader*, edited by AnaLouise Keating. Durham: Duke University Press, 2009.

Baumgartner, Alice L. *South to Freedom: Runaway Slaves to Mexico and the Road to the Civil War*. New York: Basic Books, 2020.

Beckert, Sven, and Seth Rockman. *Slavery's Capitalism: A New History of American Economic Development*. Philadelphia: University of Pennsylvania Press, 2018.

Benítez-Rojo, Antonio. *The Repeating Island: The Caribbean and the Postmodern Perspective*. Translated by James E. Maraniss. Durham: Duke University Press, 1996.

Bennett, Herman, L. *Africans in Colonial Mexico: Absolutism, Christianity, and Afro-Creole Consciousness, 1570–1640*. Bloomington: Indiana University Press, 2003.

Bergland, Renée L. *The National Uncanny: Indian Ghosts and American Subjects*. Hanover: University Press of New England, 2000.

Beverido Duhalt, Maliyel. "Estela de la Mojarra," and "Tlazoltéotl." *Museo de Antropología de Xalapa*, edited by Sara Ladrón de Guevara. Special issue of *Arqueología Mexicana* 22 (2006): 36–37, 75.

Blake, Michael. *Maize for the Gods: Unearthing the 9,000-Year History of Corn*. Berkeley: University of California Press, 2015.

A Bill to Establish an Uniform Rule of Naturalization, and Enable Aliens to Hold Lands under Certain Conditions; 3/4/1790; (SEN1A-C1); Bills and Resolutions Originating in the House and Considered in the Senate, 1789–2002; Records of the U.S. Senate, Record Group 46; National Archives Building, Washington, DC. Web. 9 December 2021.

Bloom, Harold. "Introduction." *Carlos Fuentes' The Death of Artemio Cruz*, edited by Harold Bloom, 1–3. New York: Chelsea, 2006.

Boldy, Steven. "Fathers and Sons in Fuentes' *La muerte de Artemio Cruz*." *Carlos Fuentes' The Death of Artemio Cruz*, edited by Harold Bloom, 67–80. New York: Chelsea, 2006.

Botton-Burlá, Flora. "Las coplas de 'La Llorona'." *Estudios de folklore y literature dedicados a Mercedes Diaz Roig*, edited by Beatriz Gaiza Cuarón and Yvette Jimenez de Báez, 551–72. México: El Colegio de México, 1992.

Bustamante, Jayro. Interview by Carlos Aguilar. "Crying for Justice: Jayro Bustamante on *La Llorona*. RogerEbert.com. Web. 06 August 2020.

Butler, Judith. *Precarious Life: The Power of Mourning and Violence*. London: Verso, 2003.

Cartwright, Samuel A. "Diseases and Peculiarities of the Negro Race." 1851. PBS "Africans in America." Web. 20 October 2021.

Chacón, Gloria Elizabeth. *Indigenous Cosmolectics: Kab'awil and the Making of Maya and Zapotec Literatures*. Chapel Hill: University of North Carolina Press, 2018.

Chan Briceño, Doroteo. "X-táabay." *Ja'asaj Óol, Kili'ich Kúuchilo'ob Yéetel Yumtzilo'ob II / Espantos, lugares sagrados y dioses II*, edited by Feliciano Sánchez Chan, 58–60, 70–71 Mérida: Instituto de Cultura de Yucatán, 2007.

Chinchilla Mazariegos, Oswaldo. *Art and Myth of the Ancient Maya*. New Haven: Yale University Press, 2017.

Chopin, Kate. *A Pair of Silk Stockings and Other Stories*. New York: Dover Thrift, 1996.

Christenson, Allen J., trans. *Popol Vuh: Sacred Book of the Quiché Maya People*. Norman: University of Oklahoma Press, 2003.

Cisneros, Sandra. *Woman Hollering Creek and Other Stories*. New York: Random House, 1991.

Cohn, Deborah. *History and Memory in the Two Souths: Recent Southern and Spanish American Fiction*. Nashville: Vanderbilt University Press, 1999.

Covarrubias, Miguel. *Mexico South: The Isthmus of Tehuantepec*. 1947. New York: Knopf, 1967.

Davis, Jack E. *The Gulf: The Making of an American Sea*. New York: Liveright, 2017.

Davis, Thadious. *Games of Property: Law, Race, Gender, and Faulkner's Go Down, Moses*. Durham: Duke University Press, 2003.

Díaz-Sánchez, Micaela, and Alexandro D. Hernández. "The Son Jarocho as Afro-Mexican Resistance Music." *The Journal of Pan-African Studies* 6, no. 1 (2013): 187–209.

Douglass, Frederick. *Autobiographies*. New York: Library of America. 1994.

Du Bois, W. E. B. *The Souls of Black Folk*. 1903. New York: Bantam, 1989.

Edmonson, Munro S., ed. and trans. *Heaven Born Mérida and Its Destiny: The Book of Chilam Balam of Chumayel*. Austin: University of Texas Press, 1986.

Edwards, Erica R. "Sex after the Black Normal." *Differences: A Journal of Feminist and Cultural Studies* 26, no. 1 (2015): 141–67.

Eljaiek-Rodríguez, Gabriel. *Selva de fantasmas: El gótico en la literatura y el cine latinoamericanos*. Bogotá: Pontificia Universidad Javeriana, 2017.

Esplin, Emron. "Faulkner and Latin America; Latin America in Faulkner." In *William Faulkner in Context*, edited by John T. Matthews, 270–78. New York: Cambridge University Press, 2015.

Farrier, David. *Anthropocene Poetics: Deep Time, Sacrifice Zones, and Extinction*. Minneapolis: University of Minnesota Press, 2019.

Faulkner, William. "Address upon Receiving the Nobel Prize for Literature." 1950. In *The Portable Faulkner*, edited by Malcolm Cowley, 649–50. New York: Penguin, 2003.

———. *Go Down, Moses*. 1942. New York: Vintage, 2011.

―――. "A Letter to the North: William Faulkner, the South's Foremost Writer, Warns on Integration—'Stop Now for a Moment'." *Life*, 51–52, 5 March 1956.

Flores-Silva, Dolores, and Keith Cartwright. " 'El grito de Yanga': la invitación sonora a la revuelta libertadora de México." *La Palabra y el Hombre: Revista de la Universidad Veracruzana*, no. 53, July–September, 66–71, 2020.

Ford, Sarah Gilbreath. *Haunted Property: Slavery and the Gothic.* Jackson: University Press of Mississippi, 2020.

Fortier, Alcée. *Louisiana Folk-Tales in French Dialect and English Translation.* 1895. New Orleans: Cornerstone Books, 2014.

Fuentes, Carlos. *The Death of Artemio Cruz.* 1962. Translated by Alfred MacAdam. New York: Farrar, Straus and Giroux, 2009.

Garnet, Henry Highland. "An Address to the Slaves of the United States of America." *Black Writers of America: A Comprehensive Anthology*, edited by Richard Barksdale and Keneth Kinnamon, 176–79. New York: Macmillan, 1972.

Garza Zamarripa, Lucinda. "De Misisipi a Veracruz: La influencia del gótico sureño en *Temporada de huracanes* de Fernanda Melchor." *Armas y Letras: Revista de Literatura, Arte y Cultura de la Universidad Autónoma de Nuevo León*, September 2020, 56–58. Web. 16 May 2021.

Giroux, Henry. "Reading Hurricane Katrina: Race, Class and the Biopolitics of Disposability." *College Literature* 33, no. 3 (2006): 171–96.

Glasgow, Ellen. "Heroes and Monsters." *Saturday Review of Literature*, 4 May 1935: 3–4.

Gleason, Judith. *Oya: In Praise of an African Goddess.* San Francisco: HarperCollins, 1992.

Glisant, Édouard. *Poetics of Relation.* Translated by Betsy Wing. Ann Arbor: University of Michigan Press, 1997.

―――. *Poétique de la relation.* Paris: Gallimard, 1990.

Goddu, Teresa A. *Gothic America: Narrative, History, and Nation.* New York: Columbia University Press, 1997.

Gouge, Earnest. *Totkv Mocvse / New Fire: Creek Folktales by Earnest Gouge*, edited and translated by Jack B. Martin, Margaret McKane Mauldin, and Juanita McGirt. Norman: University of Oklahoma Press, 2004.

Gray, Richard. "Inside the Dark House: William Faulkner, *Absalom, Absalom!* and Southern Gothic." Street and Crow 21–40. London: Palgrave Macmillan, 2016.

Guterl, Matthew Pratt. *American Mediterranean: Southern Slaveholders in the Age of Emancipation.* Cambridge, MA: Harvard University Press, 2008.

Hall, Gwendolyn Midlo. *Africans in Colonial Louisiana: The Development of Afro-Creole Culture in the Eighteenth Century.* Baton Rouge: Louisiana State University Press, 1992.

Harjo, Joy. "New Orleans." In *How We Became Human: New and Selected Poems: 1975–2001.* New York: Norton, 2002.

Harris, Wilson. *Selected Essays of Wilson Harris: The Unfinished Genesis of the Imagination*, edited by Andrew Bundy. New York: Routledge, 1999.

Hayden, Robert. *Collected Poems.* New York: Liveright, 1985.

Hernández Cuevas, Marco Polo. *African Mexicans and the Discourse on Modern Nation.* Lanham, MD: University Press of America, 2004.

The Holy Bible, King James Version. New York: Meridian, 1974.

Howe, LeAnne. *Choctalking on Other Realities.* San Francisco: Aunt Lute Books, 2013.

―――. "Faulkner Didn't Invent Yoknapatawpha, Everybody Knows That. So What Other Stories Do Chickasaws and Choctaws Know about Our Homelands?" *Faulkner and the Native South*, edited by Jay Watson, Annette Trefzer, and James G. Thomas Jr, 3–14. Jackson: University Press of Mississippi, 2019.

———. "The Unknown Women." In *Evidence of Red: Poems and Prose*, 9–20 Cambridge: Earthworks, 2005.

Hughes, Langston. "The Negro Speaks of Rivers." *Selected Poems of Langston Hughes*, 4 New York: Vintage, 1974.

Hurston, Zora Neale. *Mules and Men*. 1935. New York: Perennial, 1990.

Jacobs, Harriet. "Incidents in the Life of a Slave Girl". 1861. *In the Classic Slave Narratives*, Henry Louis Gates, Jr, 333–515. New York: Mentor, 1987.

Jiménez Sotero, Jairo Eduardo. "Racismo y mestzaje en la obra de José Vasconcelos." *La Palabra y el Hombre: Revista de la Universidad Veracruzana*, no. 53, July–September 2020, 45–48.

Johnson, James Weldon. *The Autobiography of an Ex-Colored Man*. 1912. New York: Dover Thrift, 1995.

Joysmith, Claire. "Cuchicheos, gritos y silencios: Transforming Sandra Cisneros' 'Woman Hollering Creek' into México y el Español." *FIAR: Forum for Interamerican Research* 5, no. 1 (April 2012). Web. 20 November. 2020.

Kesteloot, Lilyan, and Cherif Mbodj. *Contes et mythes Wolof*. Dakar: Les Nouvelles Éditions Africaines, 1983.

King, Martin Luther, Jr. "'The Impassable Gulf (The Parable of Dives and Lazarus),' Sermon at Dexter Avenue Baptist Church." The Martin Luther King, Jr. Research and Education Institute, Stanford University. Web. 20 October 2020.

———. *A Testament of Hope: The Essential Writings and Speeches of Martin Luther King Jr*, edited by James M. Washington. San Francisco: HarperCollins, 1991.

Kurnick, David. Review of *Hurricane Season*, by Fernanda Melchor. *Sydney Review of Books* 21 May 2020. Web. 06 June 2020.

Ladrón de Guevara, Sara. *Culturas del Golfo*. México: INAH, 2014.

Landers, Jane G. "Cimarrón and Citizen: African Ethnicity, Corporate Identity, and the Evolution of Free Black Towns in the Spanish Circum-Caribbean." In *Slaves, Subjects, and Subversives: Blacks in Colonial Latin America*, edited by Jane G. Landers and Barry M. Robinson, 111–45. Albuquerque: University of New Mexico Press, 2006.

Latapi, Andrés, and Claudio Vadillo López. *Historia Ambiental de la Región del Golfo de México: Del 2700 Antes del presente a la actualidad*. Beau Bassin, Mauritius: Editorial Académica Española, 2015.

Lewis, Simon L., and Mark A. Maslin. *The Human Planet: How We Created the Anthropocene*. New Haven: Yale University Press, 2018.

Limón, José. "La Llorona, the Third Legend of Greater Mexico: Cultural Symbols, Women, and the Political Unconscious." In *Between Borders: Essays in Mexicana and Chicana History*, edited by Adelaida Del Castillo. Encino, CA: Floricanto P, 1990.

La Llorona. Directed by Jayro Bustamante. La Casa de Producción, Les Films du Volcan. 2019. Shudder.

La Llorona. Directed by Ramón Peón. Eco Films, 1933. YouTube. Web. 2 April 2021.

Lloyd, Christopher. "Creaturely, Throwaway Life after Katrina: *Salvage the Bones* and *Beasts of the Southern Wild*." *South: A Scholarly Journal*, 48 no. 2 (2016): 246–64.

———. "Southern Gothic." *American Gothic Culture: An Edinburgh Companion*, edited by Joel Faflak and Jason Haslam, 79–91. Edinburgh: Edinburgh University Press, 2016.

Loichot, Valérie. *Water Graves: The Art of the Unritual in the Greater Caribbean*. Charlottesville: University of Virginia Press, 2020.

Lucas, Julian. "A Mexican Novel Conjures a Violent World Tinged with Beauty." Review of *Hurricane Season*, by Fernanda Melchor. *New York Times* 31 March 2020. Web. 05 June 2021.

Marroqui, José María. *La Llorona: cuento histórico mexicano*. México: I. Cumplido, 1887.

Melchor, Fernanda. *Hurricane Season*. Translated by Sophie Hughes. New York: New Directions, 2020.

———. Interview by Sophie Hughes. *Granta* 24 February 2020. Web. 06 June 2021.

———. *Temporada de huracanes*. México: Literatura Random House, 2017.

Mercier, Alfred. *Saint-Ybars: Masters and Slaves in Creole Louisiana*. Translated by Elizabeth A. Julian. Shreveport: Éditions Tintamarre, 2015.

Mitlich Osuna, Ana. "El gótico en la novela histórico Mexicana del siglo XIX." *Hispanet Journal* 4 (December 2011). Web. 16 May 2021.

Moreland, Richard C. "William Faulkner's 'Letter to the North,' W.E.B. Du Bois's Challenge, and *The Reivers*." *The Faulkner Journal* 30, no. 1 (2016): 79–104.

Morelos, José María. "Sentiments of the Nation." *The Mexico Reader: History, Culture, Politics*, edited by Gilbert M. Joseph and Timothy J. Henderson, 189–91. Durham: Duke University Press, 2006.

Moreno, Concepción. "Gótico tropical." *El Economista* 21 Junio 2017. Web. 07 June 2021.

Morrison, Toni. *Beloved*. 1987. New York: Vintage, 2004.

Mould, Tom. *Choctaw Tales*. Jackson: University Press of Mississippi, 2004.

Moynihan, Sinéad. "From Disposability to Recycling: William Faulkner and the New Politics of Rewriting in Jesmyn Ward's '*Salvage the Bones*.'" *Studies in the Novel* 47, no. 4 (2015): 550–67.

Muller, Dalia Antonia. "The Gulf World and Other Frameworks," *The American Historian*, 16 (May 2018), 16–23.

Ortuño, Antonio. "Entrevista con Fernanda Melchor: 'Aún había mucho que decir del trópico Negro.'" *Revista de la Universidad de México*. Julio 2020. Web. 07 June 2021.

Palomares Salas, Claudio. "Sefardismo y ficción fundacional: *La hija del judío* de Justo Sierra O'Reilly." *Bulletin of Hispanic Studies* 94, no. 2 (2017): 215–28.

Paz, Octavio. *The Labyrinth of Solitude and Other Writings*. Translated by Lysander Kemp, Yara Milos and Rachel Phillips Belash. New York: Grove, 1985.

Perez, Domino Renee. *There Was a Woman: La Llorona from Folklore to Popular Culture*. Austin: University of Texas Press, 2008.

Philip, Neil. *Horse Hooves and Chicken Feet: Mexican Folktales*. New York: Clarion Books, 2003.

Pinkola Estés, Clarissa. *Women Who Run with the Wolves: Myths and Stories of the Wild Woman Archetype*. New York: Ballantine, 1992.

Power, Susan. *Early Art of the Southeastern Indians: Feathered Serpents and Winged Beings*. Athens: University of Georgia Press, 2004.

Recinos, Adrián, Delia Goetz, and Sylvanus G. Morley, translators. *Popol Vuh: The Sacred Book of the Ancient Quiché Maya*. Norman: University of Oklahoma Press, 1950.

Redding, Arthur. "Ethno-gothic: Repurposing Genre in Contemporary American Literature." *American Gothic Culture: An Edinburgh Companion*, edited by Jason Haslam and Joel Faflak, 60–75. Edinburgh: Edinburgh University Press, 2016.

Richardson, Riché. "Beyoncé's South and a 'Formation' Nation." In *Beyoncé in the World: Making Meaning with Queen Bey in Troubled Times*, edited by Christina Baade and Kristin McGee, 89–109. Middleton, CT: Wesleyan University Press, 2021.

Riquelme, John Paul. Introduction. *Gothic and Modernism: Essaying Dark Literary Modernity*, edited by John Paul Riquelme, 1–23. Baltimore: Johns Hopkins University Press, 2008.

Riva Palacio, Vicente, Manuel Payno, Juan A. Mateos, and Rafael Martínez de la Torre. *El Libro Rojo 1520–1867*. London: Forgotten Books, 2017.

Rivera Garza, Cristina. *Grieving: Dispatches from a Wounded Country.* Translated by Sarah Booker. New York: The Feminist Press, 2020.

Sahagún, Fray Bernardino de. *Florentine Codex: General History of the Things of New Spain,* Book 1. Translated by Arthur J. O. Anderson and Charles E. Dibble. Salt Lake City: University of Utah Press, 1981.

———. *Florentine Codex: General History of the Things of New Spain,* Book 8. Translated by Arthur J. O. Anderson and Charles E. Dibble. Salt Lake City: University of Utah Press, 2012.

Sánchez Chan, Feliciano. "Xko' Óolal Xtáabay" / "Seductora Xtáabay." *Yaamaj yáanal Cháak / Amor bajo la lluvia.* Mérida: Conaculta, 2014. 41, 99.

Sánchez Fernández, José Roberto. *Bailes y sones deshonestos en la Nueva España.* Veracruz: Instituto Veracruzana de Cultura, 1998.

Sensibar, Judith. *Faulkner and Love: The Women Who Shaped His Art.* New Haven: Yale University Press, 2009.

Siemens, Alfred H. *Between the Summit and the Sea: Central Veracruz in the Nineteenth Century.* Vancouver: University of British Columbia Press, 1990.

Sierra O'Reilly, Justo. *La hija del judío,* edited by Manuel Sol. México: Universidad Veracruzana, 2008.

Silko, Leslie Marmon. *Storyteller.* New York: Arcade, 1981.

Sorhegui, Arturo. "La Habana-Veracruz: El Mediterráneo Americano y el circuito imperial hispano 1519–1821." *La Habana / Veracruz, Veracruz / La Habana: Las dos orillas,* edited by Bernardo García Díaz and Sergio Guerra Vilaboy, 23–43. México: Universidad Veracruzana, 2002.

Soyinka, Wole. *Myth, Literature and the African World.* 1976. New York: Cambridge University Press, 1995.

Street, Susan Castillo, and Charles L. Crow, eds. *The Palgrave Handbook of the Southern Gothic.* London: Palgrave Macmillan, 2016.

Sundquist, Erc. "Faulkner, Race, and the Forms of American Fiction." *Faulkner and Race: Faulkner and Yoknapatawpha 1986,* edited by Doreen Fowler and Ann J. Abadie. Jackson: University Press of Mississippi, 1987.

Taub, Karl. "Lightning Celts and Corn Fetishes: The Formative Olmec and the Development of Maize Symbolism in Mesoamerica and the American Southwest." *Olmec Art and Archaeology in Mesoamerica,* edited by John E. Clark and Mary E. Pye, 296–331. New Haven: Yale University Press, 2000.

Tedlock, Dennis, trans. *Popul Vuh: The Mayan Book of the Dawn of Life.* New York: Touchstone, 1996.

———. *2000 Years of Mayan Literature.* Berkeley: University of California Press, 2010.

Tamez, Margo. "My Mother Returns to Calaboz." *When the Light of the World Was Subdued, Our Songs Came Through,* edited by Joy Harjo et al. New York: Norton, 2020. 321–23.

Trump, Donald J. "Here's Donald Trump's Presidential Announcement Speech." *Time,* 16 June 2015. Web. 22 October 2021.

United States Constitution. Art. I, Sec. 2; Art. I, Sec. 9; Art. IV, Sec. 2.

United States Supreme Court, et al. *The case of Dred Scott in the United States Supreme Court. The full opinions of Chief Justice Taney and Justice Curtis, and abstracts of the opinions of the other judges; with an analysis of the points ruled, and some concluding observations.* New York, H. Greeley & co, 1860. PDF. Retrieved from the Library of Congress, <www.loc.gov/item/10034357/>. Web. 21 June 2020.

Vail, Gabrielle and Anthony Aveni. *The Madrid Codex: New Approaches to Understanding an Ancient Maya Manuscript.* Boulder: University Press of Colorado, 2004.

Vasconcelos, José. *The Cosmic Race / La raza cósmica.* Baltimore: Johns Hopkins University Press, 1997.

Vega, El Inca Garcilaso de la. *The Florida of the Inca.* Translated by John Grier Varner and Jeanette Johnson Varner. Austin: University of Texas Press, 1986.

Walcott, Derek. "The Gulf." *Collected Poems, 1948–1984.* New York: Farrar, Straus and Giroux, 1986.

Ward, Jesmyn. "Raising a black son in the U.S.: 'He had never taken a breath, and I was already mourning him.'" *The Guardian* 28 October 2017. Web. 10 October 2021.

———. *Salvage the Bones.* New York: Bloomsbury, 2011.

Watson, Jay. "So Easy Even a Child Can Do It: William Faulkner's Southern Gothicizers." *Mississippi Quarterly* 72, no. 1 (2019): 1–24.

———. *William Faulkner and the Faces of Modernity.* Oxford: Oxford University Press, 2019.

Weaver, Jace. "Splitting the Earth: First Utterances and Pluralist Separatism." *Native American Literary Nationalism*, edited by Jace C Weaver, Craig S. Womack, and Robert Warrior, 1–89. Albuquerque: University of New Mexico Press, 2006.

———. *That People Might Live: Native American Literatures and Native American Community.* New York: Oxford University Press, 1997.

White, Nancy Marie, ed. *Gulf Coast Archaeology: The Southeastern United States and Mexico.* Gainesville: University Press of Florida, 2005.

Worley, Paul M. and Rita M. Palcios. *Unwriting Maya Literature: Ts'íib as Recorded Knowledge.* Tucson: University of Arizona Press, 2019.

Wyllie, Cherra. "The mural paintings of El Zapotal, Veracruz, Mexico." *Ancient Mesoamerica* 21, no. 2 (2010): 209–27.

———. "In Search of Tamazunchale." *The Huasteca: Culture, History, and Interregional Exchange*, edited by Katherine A. Faust and Kim N. Richter, 168–94. Norman: University of Oklahoma Press, 2015.

Yaeger, Patricia. *Dirt and Desire: Reconstructing Southern Women's Writing, 1930–1990.* Chicago: University of Chicago Press, 2000.

INDEX

Lightning Source UK Ltd.
Milton Keynes UK
UKHW021805211022
410881UK00001B/105